W9-ATK-643

REA's Books Are The Best...
They have rescued lots of grades and more!

(a sample of the <u>hundreds of letters</u> REA receives each year)

"Your books are great! They are very helpful, and have upped my grade in every class. Thank you for such a great product."

Student, Seattle, WA

"Your book has really helped me sharpen my skills and improve my weak areas. Definitely will buy more."

Student, Buffalo, NY

"Compared to the other books that my fellow students had, your book was the most useful in helping me get a great score."

Student, North Hollywood, CA

"I really appreciate the help from your excellent book. Please keep up your great work."

Student, Albuquerque, NM

"Your book was such a better value and was so much more complete than anything your competition has produced (and I have them all)!"

Teacher, Virginia Beach, VA

(more on next page)

(continued from previous page)

" Your books have saved my GPA, and quite possibly my sanity. My course grade is now an 'A', and I couldn't be happier. "

Student, Winchester, IN

" These books are the best review books on the market. They are fantastic! "

Student, New Orleans, LA

" Your book was responsible for my success on the exam. . . I will look for REA the next time I need help. "

Student, Chesterfield, MO

" I think it is the greatest study guide I have ever used! "

Student, Anchorage, AK

" I encourage others to buy REA because of their superiority. Please continue to produce the best quality books on the market. "

Student, San Jose, CA

" Just a short note to say thanks for the great support your book gave me in helping me pass the test . . . I'm on my way to a B.S. degree because of you ! "

Student, Orlando, FL

FRENCH

By the Staff of
Research & Education Association

Research & Education Association
Visit our website at
www.rea.com

Research & Education Association
61 Ethel Road West
Piscataway, New Jersey 08854
E-mail: info@rea.com

SUPER REVIEW®
OF FRENCH

Year 2006 Printing

Printed in the United States of America

Library of Congress Control Number 00-130291

International Standard Book Number 0-87891-187-1

SUPER REVIEW® and REA® are registered trademarks of
Research & Education Association, Inc.

What this Super Review® Will Do for You

REA's Super Review provides **all you need to know** to excel in class and succeed on midterms, finals, and even pop quizzes.

Think of this book as giving you access to your own private tutor. Here, right at your fingertips, is a brisk review to help you not only understand your textbook but also pick up where even some of the best lectures leave off.

Outstanding **Super Review** features include...

- Comprehensive yet concise coverage
- Targeted preparation for subject tests
- Easy-to-follow **Q** & **A** format that helps you master the subject matter
- End-of-chapter quizzes that provide pretest tune-up

We think you'll agree that, whether you're prepping for your next test or want to be a stronger contributor in class, **REA's Super Review** truly provides **all you need to know!**

Larry B. Kling
Super Review Program Director

CONTENTS

4   NOUNS AND ARTICLES

5   THE PARTITIVE ARTICLE (*LE PARTITIF*)

6   ADJECTIVES

7   PRONOUNS

8   VERBS

CHAPTER 1

The Sounds of French

1.1 Pronunciation Hints

French is one of the Romance languages (the others are Spanish, Italian, Portuguese, Romanian, Catalan, and Provençal) and is "vocalic" in its sound, i.e., based on vowels. This structure gives the language its soft and flowing character. English speakers can attain good pronunciation if the following simple rules are kept in mind:

- There are **no diphthongs** in French, as there are in English: "boy" = "baw," "ee," "yuh." French vowels are clean and pure; e.g., *imiter* = "ee-mee-tay" (to imitate) and should be formed without any secondary movement of the jaw.

- Every syllable is of **equal importance** in volume and stress; e.g., English: de/VEL/op/ment and French: *dé/ve/lop/pe/ment.* There is a slight emphasis on the last syllable in words of two or more syllables and in a group of words: *dé/li/CIEUX; Je parle franÇAIS;* but it is not a strong stress.

- Consonants are **softened:** don't "explode" your d's, t's, b's, p's, g's, and k's and your accent will improve.

- There are **two sounds** that are generally difficult for English speakers: the "r," which can be achieved by "gargling," and the "u" (as in *tu*), which is made by puckering your lips as if to whistle, while you say "ee."

1.1.1 Further Pronunciation Details

French has the same alphabet as English; some letters are written but are not pronounced (e.g., most final consonants: *sans, chez, tard, livres*). Exceptions to this rule are the final "c," as in *bouc* (billy goat), "f," as in *chef* (head, chief), "l," as in *formel* (formal), and "r," as in *air.*

Also silent are "h," as in *homme, héros, théâtre,* and some combinations of letters, as in *parlent, monsieur, voudraient.*

In cognates (words that we recognize from English), spelling is often different from English, with letters added, deleted or changed, giving the word a "French" look: *classe, indépendance, appartement, université.* The International Phonetic Alphabet (IPA), utilized in most good dictionaries, will help you understand the sounds of French vowels, which remain unchanged, even in different spelling groups.

1.2 The International Phonetic Alphabet (IPA)

There are 17 consonants, 16 vowels (12 oral vowels pronounced in the mouth and 4 oral vowels articulated in the nasal passage), and 3 semi-vowels/semi-consonants halfway between vowels and consonants. These sounds are expressed by phonetic symbols which are always written between [ ].

1.2.1 Oral Vowels

Phonetic Symbol	French Example	English Approx.	Remarks
1. [a]	*avec*	Ah!	Open your mouth.
2. [ɑ]	*pâle*	Ahh!	Longer than [a].
3. [e]	*été*	say	Don't add "yuh."
4. [ɛ]	*elle*	elf	More open than [e].
5. [i]	*ici*	see	Smile; don't add "yuh."
6. [o]	*mot*	Moe	Don't add "wuh."
7. [ɔ]	*porte*	up	More open than [o].
8. [ø]	*peu*	put	Lips very rounded.
9. [œ]	*sœur*	purr	More open than [ø].

10. [u]	*nous*	noose	Don't add "wuh."
11. [y]	*tu*	No English equivalent	Round your lips as if to whistle while saying "ee."
12. [ə]	*je*	wood	Resembles [ø] but is much shorter: mute "e."

1.2.2 Nasal Vowels

Phonetic Symbol	French Example	English Approx.	Remarks
1. [ɑ̃]	*sans*	on	Say "on" with your mouth open.
2. [ɛ̃]	*pain*	can	Say "can" with your mouth open.
3. [ɔ̃]	*bon*	own	Say "own" with your mouth open.
4. [œ̃]	*un*	fun	Say "fun" with your mouth open.

Remember this little phrase, which includes all the nasal vowels: ***Un bon vin blanc*** [œ̃ bɔ̃ vɛ̃ blɑ̃]. (A good white wine.)

Denasalization, or **oral** pronunciation, of the nasal vowel occurs under **two** conditions:

1. When a nasal vowel **is followed by another "n" or "m"**: e.g., *intime* [ɛ̃tim]; *innocent* [inɔsɑ̃]; *important* [ɛ̃pɔrtɑ̃]; *immédiat* [imedja]; *enfant* [ɑ̃fɑ̃]; *ennemi* [ɛnmi]; *bon* [bɔ̃]; *bonne* [bɔn].

2. When a nasal vowel **is followed by another vowel:** e.g., *pain* [pɛ̃]; *peine* [pɛn]; *incident* [ɛ̃sidɑ̃]; *inutile* [inytil]; *profond* [prɔfɔ̃]; *chronique* [krɔnik].

1.2.3 Semi-Vowels/Semi-Consonants: Halfway between Vowels and Consonants

1. [j] *soulier* [sulje]; *bien* [bjɛ̃]; *hier* [jɛr]. ([j] is like biblical "Yea.")

2. [w] *mois* [mwa]; *Louis* [lwi]; *ouest* [wɛst]; *ouïr* [wir]; *soir* [swar].

3. [ɥ] *huit* [ɥit]; *lui* [lɥi]; *cuisine* [kɥizin]. (Based on [y] + [i]; very closed.)

1.2.4 Consonants

Pronounce them softly!

Bi-labials: [p], [b], [m]. Both lips are used. *Papa, bébé, maman.*

Labio-dentals: [f], [v]. Teeth against lower lip. *Frère, vie.*

Dentals: [t], [d], [n], [l]. Put your tongue against the back of your upper teeth to soften the sound. Don't "explode" it! *Ton, de, non, la.*

Alveolars: [ʃ], [ʒ]. Air is forced between upper and lower teeth. [ʃ] *chanson, riche, acheter;* [ʒ] *Jean, Giverny, voyage.* In English: **she**, plea**s**ure.

Palatal: [ɲ] "N" + yuh. *Champagne, Allemagne.* In English: He'll train **yuh.**

Velars: [k], [g]. Produced in the throat; make them soft. [k] *avec, qui, klaxon;* [g] *grand, fatigué.*

Uvular: [r]. Gargle it! *rue, Robert, travail.*

1.2.5 Spelling Groups

Phonetic symbols and examples of some common **spelling** combinations:

[e] é = *école;* ée = *fiancée;* ef = *clef* or *clé;* er = *chanter;* es = *ces;* et = *cadet;* ez = *nez;* ai = *j'ai;* e + il or ille = *pareil, merveille;* ay = *ayons.*

[ɛ] ai + consonant = *aide, aile, j'aime, palais, caisse, chaise, paix, faites;* è = *père; chèque, mène, achète, Thèbes, mèche, il lève;* ê = *tête, même, guêpe, gêne, chaîne;* e + tte = *dette;* e + l or lle = *sel, elle;* e + ige = *neige;* e + ine = *peine.*

[i] *ami, il y a.*

[o] *tôt, sauce, beau, ôter*

[ote] *haut.*

[ɔ] *porte, observer* (most words with initial "o" are pronounced [ɔ]).

[œ] *cœur, peur, jeune, beurre, seul, deuil* [dœj], *bœuf.*

[u] *trou, toute, vous.*

[y] *vue, rhume* [rym], *utile* [ytil].

[ə] *je, demain, menace* [mənas], *fenêtre* [fənɛtrə].

1.3 The French Alphabet

Here is the phonetic pronunciation of the French alphabet:

Letter	Name	As in...
a	[a]	*parc*
b	[be]	*belle*
c	[se]	*ici*
d	[de]	*dame*
e	[ə]	*école* = [ekɔl]; *père* = [pɛr]; *le* = [lə]
f	[ɛf]	*faire*
g[1]	[ʒe]	*gare; gomme; guerre; général; gilet*
h[2]	[aʃ]	*habiter* = [abite]; **héros* = ['ero]. The * and ' indicate an aspirate "h," one which is not linked to a preceding consonant.
i	[i]	*idée; imiter* = [imite]; *inégal* = [inegal]; *ici; il y a; innocent* = [inɔsã]; *mystérieux*
j[1]	[ʒi]	*jeune*
k	[ka]	*kilo.* Very few French words begin with "k"; most that do are borrowed foreign words.
l	[ɛl]	*laver; ville*[3] = [vil]; *famille* = [famij]
m	[ɛm]	*mardi; ami*
n	[ɛn]	*noble; initial; animé*
o	[o]	*dormir; œuf* = [œf]
p	[pe]	*papa*
q	[ky]	*question* = [kɛstjõ]

r	[ɛr]	*rire; pardon; irréel*
s	[ɛs]	*salle* = [sal]; *rester* = [rɛste]; *lisse* = [lis]: Initial "s;" "s" before a consonant, and double "s" are pronounced "s." *Plaisir* = [plezir]: "s" between two vowels = [z].
t	[te]	*tête; fait*[4]
u	[y]	*utile; tu*
v	[ve]	*voix* = [vwa]; *arriver*
w	[dubləve]	*walkman* = [wɔkman]; *wagon* = [vagɔ̃]. Many foreign words with an initial "w" are used in French. Some are pronounced "v" and some "w."
x	[ix]	Relatively few words have this initial letter.
y	[igrɛk]	Relatively few words have this initial letter.
z	[zɛd]	Relatively few words have this initial letter.

Note:

[1] "G" and "J": "g" is called [ʒe] (like "jay" in English) and "j" is called [ʒi] like "gee" in English. Remember that the names of these two letters are the opposite of what they are in the English alphabet.

[2] Aspirate "h" is not linked to a preceding consonant. Consider *"les héros"* [le ero]; if you link these words, the result is [lezero] (*"les zéros"*) and that is certainly not the usual intention when talking about heroes!

[3] Three words and their derivatives that end in *"-ille"* are pronounced [il]: *mille, villes, tranquillé* [mil vil trãkil]. Similarly pronounced are *million, milliard,* and *village. Lille* (the city) is also [lil].

[4] Sometimes the final "t" is pronounced: *C'est un fait.* [fet] or [fe].

1.4 Accents

Accents are used in French to indicate pronunciation of vowels or to differentiate between homonyms (two words that sound alike but have different meanings, e.g., *où/ou; la/là*).

é = *accent aigu* (acute) is used only on closed "e" [e] and sounds approximately like "a" in the English word "say": *éléphant, médecin* [medsɛ̃], *j'ai chanté, je suis désolé.*

è = *accent grave* is used to give the sound of open "e" [ɛ] to a mute "e" [ə] that stands before a consonant and is followed by another mute "e": The open "e" of the accent grave sounds approximately like the "e" in the English word "elf": *père, sèche, Hélène, j'achète, deuxième.*

à, ù = *accent grave* is used to make a distinction between two words that are spelled alike but have different meanings. There is no difference in the pronunciation of these two words: *à Paris/ Pierre a une voiture; la femme/là-bas* (over there); *Où est Jean?/ Marie ou Simone* (or).

ç = *cédille* is used only on a "c" so it is pronounced [s] before "a," "o," and "u" and sounds approximately like "s" in the English word "sun": *ça, garçon, je suis déçu.*

ä, ë, ï, ö, ü = *le tréma* is used on the second vowel when two vowels occur together, to indicate that they are to be pronounced separately: *haïr* [air]; *aïeux* [ajø]; *Noël.*

Problem Solving Examples:

Select the correct word form in parentheses:

1. *Pourriez-vous me dire (**où, ou**) je peux trouver une bonne boulangerie (**où, ou**) un bon supermarché?*

2. *J'aimerais bien rester (**la, là**) pendant que vous allez à la pâtisserie. Je ne veux pas quitter (**la, là**) maison.*

1. *Pourriez-vous me dire **où** je peux trouver une bonne boulangerie **ou** un bon supermarché?*

2. *J'aimerais bien rester **là** pendant que vous allez à la pâtisserie. Je ne veux pas quitter **la** maison.*

In sentence 1, "*où*" is selected the first time because with an accent *grave* it means "where." "*Ou*" is selected the second time because without an accent *grave* it means "or." In sentence 2, "*là*" is selected the first time because with an accent *grave* it means "here." "*La*" is selected the second time because without an accent *grave* it is a feminine definite article meaning "the," and "*maison*" (house) is feminine.

Correct the following sentences by inserting the proper accents:

1. *Le pere et la mere de Patrick partent en vacances sans lui—il est tres decu, mais, il va rester avec son frere a la campagne.*

2. *Je ne vais pas a l'ecole pendant les vacances de Noel.*

3. *Ma mere est tres fatiguee; elle a passé une nuit blanche.*

1. *Le père et la mère de Patrick partent en vacances sans lui—il est très déçu, mais, il va rester avec son frère à la campagne.*

2. *Je ne vais pas à l'école pendant les vacances de Noël.*

3. *Ma mère est très fatiguée; elle a passé une nuit blanche.*

1.5   Liaison

Liaison, or linking, occurs in speaking when a final consonant precedes an initial vowel or an "h": *cet homme; vous êtes; nos amies; un anniversaire; un bel arbre; le bouc émissaire; un grand orchestre; un patron ambitieux.*

1.5.1   Some Liaisons Are to Be Avoided

- Never link *"et"* to a following vowel: *Un chapeau et/un livre.*

- Never link a final "s" to an aspirate "h": *les/hors-d'œuvre* [le ɔrdœvrə].

- But do link the "h" in: *un hôpital, l'homme, des huîtres,* etc.

- In inversions, don't link the final "s" of the plural to a following vowel: *Avez-vous/une sœur? Vont-ils/en Europe? Sont-elles/ ici?* In fact, the tendency among many young French speakers today is to avoid liaison, except where it is necessary for comprehension.

1.6 Elision

When final and initial vowels come together, the final vowel is replaced by an apostrophe: *l'amie, c'est; l'examen; il n'est pas; l'heure; Est-ce qu'il faut parler?*

"*Si*" is elided before "i" but not before the other vowels: *s'il vous plaît; si elle accepte; si on arrive,* etc.

1.7 Syllabification

A French syllable is determined by the vowel within it: *é-té; a-mi; dé-ter-mi-ner; ré-pé-ti-tion; in-di-vi-du,* etc. When you wish to separate a word, either do so at the vowel itself, or if there is a double consonant, make the separation between the two letters: *fi-nis-sez; lit-té-ra-ture; syl-la-be,* etc.

Exceptions: *le huit octobre; le onze février, tu as, tu es, Le Havre.*

CHAPTER 2

Cognates — Words You Recognize

2.1 Cognates Common to Both Languages

Many words are common to both French and English. Others have slight spelling differences, and still others have familiar characteristics that help to identify their meaning.

restaurant	*dessert*	*menu*	*service*	*table*
art	*culture*	*film*	*statue*	*tennis*
football	*sport*	*machine*	*science*	*client*
magazine	*concert*	*piano*	*cousin*	*parents*
rouge	*rose*	*violet*	*orange*	*automobile*
route	*train*	*promenade*	*taxi*	*suite*
voyage	*probable*	*possible*	*solitude*	*surprise*
courage	*brave*	*moment*	*content*	*secret*

2.2 Cognates with Minor Spelling Changes

These common words are spelled differently from their English cognates and may cause confusion:

musique	*théâtre*	*touriste*	*personne*
fascinant	*magique*	*comédie*	*congrès*
exercice	*dictionnaire*	*allée*	*bleu*
sénateur	*thé*	*chrysanthème*	*acteur*

hôtel	*démocratie*	*adresse*	*personnage*
opéra	*leçon*	*élection*	*omelette*
appartement	*élégant*	*artiste*	*américain*
indépendant	*revue*	*mémoire*	*auteur*
gouvernement	*rime*	*automne*	*saison*
tragédie	*nationalité*	*intéressant*	*couleur*
répéter	*pourpre*	*voter*	*douzaine*
succès	*actrice*	*président*	*loyauté*
riz	*oignon*	*chambre*	*classe*
distingué	*calendrier*	*médecin*	*difficulté*
poème	*télévision*	*mathématiques*	*peintre*
professeur	*poète*	*exemple*	*mariage*
erreur	*sophistiqué*	*première*	*rythme*
littérature	*danseur*	*procès*	*carotte*

2.3 *Faux Amis* (False Friends)

The following cognates seem to mean one thing in English but really mean something quite different in French:

à l'heure – at the present time

actuellement – now

assister – to attend

se douter de – to suspect

ignorer – to be unaware of

bague – ring (noun)

une occasion – an opportunity, a chance

les actualités – the news

en réalité – actually

attendre – to wait for

sans doute – probably

large – broad, wide

sac – bag, purse (noun)

place – a square (Place Vendome) or a seat at the theatre, etc. (noun)

regarder – to look at, to gaze at

chargé – loaded, burdened

rester – to stay or remain

sensiblement – approximately

librairie – book store (noun)

roman – novel (noun)

voyage – journey (noun)

quitter – to leave

crier – to shout or yell

sensible – sensitive, keen senses

canapé – sofa, couch (noun)

bibliothèque – library (noun)

journée – all day long (noun)

voyager – to travel

travailler – to work

Problem Solving Example:

Select the correct word in parentheses. Avoid the *faux amis*.

1. *J'ai trouvé mon portefeuille dans (**ma bague, mon sac**).*
2. *Nous allons faire (**une journée, un voyage**) lundi prochain.*
3. *Est-ce que vous avez faim?*
   *- Non, (**actuellement, en réalité**), j'ai déjà mangé.*
4. *On peut acheter un livre dans (**une librairie, une bibliothèque**).*

1. *J'ai trouvé mon portefeuille dans **mon sac**.*
2. *Nous allons faire **un voyage** lundi prochain.*
3. *Est-ce que vous avez faim?*
   *- Non, **en réalité**, j'ai déjà mangé.*
4. *On peut acheter un livre dans **une librairie**.*

In sentence 1, *mon sac* is the only correct answer because *ma bague* is a faux ami that means "ring" in French. *Une journée* is the correct answer for sentence 2 because it means "all day long" in French, not "a journey" as it means in English. In sentence 3 *en réalité*, which means "actually," is correct because *actuellement* is a *faux ami* that means "now" in French.

2.4   Some Borrowed Words

Some words that have been borrowed from French have been "Americanized," in that their pronunciation has changed somewhat. These words include:

la lingerie	*la chaise longue*	*le quai*
le maître d'hôtel	*la femme*	*à la mode*
le salon	*hors-d'œuvre*	*le foyer*
le billet doux	*à la carte*	*le grand prix*
le chef-d'oeuvre	*tête-à-tête*	*le rendez-vous*
le café	*la haute couture*	*le chauffeur*
le garage	*la cuisine*	*le croissant*
la vinaigrette	*la détente*	*le coup d'état*

le chiffon	*mot-clef*	*le tour de force*
la liaison	*de luxe*	*exposé*
le gourmet	*rouge*	*au pair*
chic	*le coup de grâce*	*fiancé(e)*
beau	*le soufflé*	*voilà*
le fait accompli	*la fête*	*l'idiot savant*
la suite	*la raison d'être*	*en garde*
le ballet	*le pas de deux*	*l'entrepreneur*

French has borrowed many words from English, too. (It's *"le franglais"* that purists deplore!)

le week-end	*le parking*	*faire du shopping*
les fast-foods	*le steak*	*la jet-set*
un job	*"cool"*	*"super-cool"*
les spots télévisés	*faire du foot*	*les stars*
le rock and roll	*le marketing*	*le business*
le budget	*un manager*	*le "look"*
la "pub"[licité]	*le tunnel*	*un building de haut standing*
un superman	*un speaker*	*une speakerine*

2.5 Capitalization

Fewer words are capitalized in French than in English. Important examples are:

"*Je*" is capitalized only when it begins a sentence: *Je suis son ami.* But: *Ce matin, je vais rester ici. Elle sait que je veux partir. Que sais-je? Il faut que je te parle. Je vais au cinéma et je vais acheter deux billets.*

Names of languages are not capitalized: *le français, le chinois, le russe, l'italien, l'anglais, le grec, l'allemand, le japonais.*

Days of the week and months of the year are not capitalized: *lundi, mardi, mercredi, dimanche; janvier, avril, décembre.*

Nationalities of people or national origins of things (adjectives) are not capitalized: *Vous êtes américain(e). Elle a une voiture danoise. J'aime la cuisine chinoise. Gildas est breton. Margot porte une robe parisienne.*

Nationalities (people) are capitalized: *Les Suisses font du chocolat magnifique. Connais-tu des Français? On croit que les Américains sont riches. Les Canadiens sont nos voisins. Nous avons rencontré beaucoup d'Européens.*

Names of cities, states, provinces, countries, rivers, oceans, mountains, and continents are capitalized: *Londres, la Californie, la Normandie, l'Italie, les États-Unis, l'Asie, l'Australie, la Seine, l'Atlantique, les Alpes.*

Capitalization varies for the titles of books, films, or plays: Generally the article is not capitalized but the first noun is: *l'Etranger; les Misérables; le Rouge et le noir; les Fleurs du mal.* But when the first word is not an article, only that word is capitalized: *Lettres de mon moulin; Tous les matins du monde; Autant en emporte le vent* (Gone with the Wind). When the title is a clause and begins with a definite article, that is the capitalized word: *Les dieux ont soif; La guerre de Troie n'aura pas lieu; Le deuil sied à Electra* (Mourning Becomes Electra).

Problem Solving Example:

 Correct the following passage using correct spelling, meaning, and capitalization:

> *Je voudrais faire une journée aux états-unis ou en asie. Je sais qu'il y a beaucoup d'artiste et de touriste à New York. J'aime bien la cuisine Chinoise. Mais je ne peux pas ignorer qu'elle coûte cher et qu'il va falloir d'abord gagner un peu d'argent.*

 *Je voudrais faire **un voyage aux États-Unis** ou en **Asie**. Je sais qu'il y a **beaucoup d'artistes** et de **touristes** à New York. J'aime bien la cuisine **chinoise**. Mais je ne peux pas **nier** qu'elle coûte cher et qu'il va falloir d'abord gagner un peu d'argent.*

Voyage should be used instead of *journée*, since journeé is a *faux ami* meaning "day." *États-Unis* (United States) and *Asie* (Asia) are continents and as in English, are always capitalized. *Beaucoup* is the correct spelling for "much," or in this case "many." "*Artistes*" and "*touristes*"

take the plural because we are saying *"beaucoup,"* which means "many." The nationality *"chinoise"* should not be capitalized because nationalities and origins in French are not capitalized. *"Ignorer"* would not be a good word to use in this case because it means to be unaware of something. *"Nier"* is a better choice because it means "to deny."

2.5.1 Interrogative Sentences

Questions are usually formed most simply by adding *Est ce-que?* to a declarative sentence:

Est-ce que Robert lit beaucoup? Does Robert read a lot?

Est-ce que tu veux aller avec nous? Do you want to go with us?

Est-ce que l'enfant sait lire? Does the child know how to read?

Questions are also formed by **inversion**, i.e., placing the verb **before** the **subject**:

Buvez-vous trop de café? Do you drink too much coffee?

Avons-nous les billets? Do we have the tickets?

Travailles-tu maintenant? Are you working now?

Note: When the subject is in the third person, **name the subject** and **then invert the verb-pronoun** for a question:

Ces femmes ont-elles assez d'argent? Do these women have enough money?

La guerre est-elle nécessaire? Is war necessary?

Sylvie prépare-t-elle un grand dîner? Is Sylvie making a big dinner?

Note: Sometimes when using inversion when the pronoun that is joined to the verb begins with a vowel and the verb itself has no strong ending consonants to pronounce, an extra "t" is added for the sake of pronunciation.

Sylvie prépare-t-elle un grand dîner? Is Sylvie making a big dinner?

A-t-il une grande famille? Does he have a big family?

A-t-on des cahiers? Does everyone have notebooks?

The "t" does not change the meaning of the sentence, but simply makes it easier to pronounce vowel sounds together.

Problem Solving Example:

Using the infinitive form of the verb given in capital letters, replace the infinitive with the correct conjugated verb form in the present tense.

> *Lucienne ne FAIRE jamais ses devoirs. Mais, aujourd'hui elle DECIDER de rester chez elle pour finir ses devoirs. Ses amies Margot et Juliette ALLER au cinéma. Le film <u>Tous les matins du monde</u> ÊTRE populaire en ce moment. Lucienne VOULOIR aller au cinéma aussi. Elle n'AIMER pas rester chez elle mais elle DEVOIR le faire. Elle COMPRENDRE maintenant qu'il ÊTRE nécessaire de faire ses devoirs. Elle SAVOIR qu'elle ne POUVOIR pas sortir avec ses amies.*

> *Lucienne ne **fait** jamais ses devoirs. Mais, aujourd'hui elle **décide** de rester chez elle pour finir ses devoirs. Ses amies Margot et Juliette **vont** au cinéma. Le film <u>Tous les matins du monde</u> **est** populaire en ce moment. Lucienne **veut** aller au cinéma aussi. Elle n'**aime** pas rester chez elle mais elle **doit** le faire. Elle **comprend** qu'il **est** nécessaire de faire ses devoirs. Elle **sait** qu'elle ne **peut** pas sortir avec ses amies.*

CHAPTER 3

By the Numbers

3.1 Counting from 1 to 1,000,000,000

The French numerical system becomes somewhat complicated when you arrive at the 70's, 80's, and 90's. Otherwise the pattern of counting is regular:

un	[œ̃]	1	*onze*	[ɔ̃z]	11
deux	[dø]	2	*douze*	[duz]	12
trois	[trwa]	3	*treize*	[trɛz]	13
quatre	[katrə]	4	*quatorze*	[katɔrz]	14
cinq	[sɛ̃k]	5	*quinze*	[kɛ̃z]	15
six	[sis]	6	*seize*	[sɛz]	16
sept	[sɛt]	7	*dix-sept*	[disɛt]	17
huit	[ɥit]	8	*dix-huit*	[dizɥit]	18
neuf	[nœf]	9	*dix-neuf*	[diznœf]	19
dix	[dis]	10	*vingt*	[vɛ̃]	20

vingt et un	21	*vingt-sept*	27
vingt-deux	22	*vingt-huit*	28
vingt-trois	23	*vingt-neuf*	29
vingt-quatre	24	*trente* [trɑ̃t]	30
vingt-cinq	25		
vingt-six	26		

Continue the same pattern with:

trente et un, trente-deux, etc. 31, 32, . . .
quarante, quarante et un, quarante-deux, etc. 40, 41, 42, . . .
cinquante, cinquante et un, cinquante-deux, etc. 50, 51, 52, . . .

Note: Continue with *soixante, soixante et un* (60, 61) until you reach *soixante-neuf* (69). Now you will say 60 + 10, *soixante-dix,* for 70. After *dix,* continue with *onze,* so that you say:

soixante-dix	70	*soixante-quinze*	75
soixante et onze	71	*soixante-seize*	76
soixante-douze	72	*soixante-dix-sept*	77
soixante-treize	73	*soixante-dix-huit*	78
soixante-quatorze	74	*soixante-dix-neuf*	79

Now you are going to **multiply: 4×20 = *quatre* $\times$ *vingts* = *quatre-vingts*** (80). Note that there is an **"s"** in *quatre-vingts* and that there is **no "s"** and **no "et"** in *quatre-vingt-un* (81).

Now continue with *–deux:*

quatre-vingt-deux	82	*quatre-vingt-six*	86
quatre-vingt-trois	83	*quatre-vingt-sept*	87
quatre-vingt-quatre	84	*quatre-vingt-huit*	88
quatre-vingt-cinq	85	*quatre-vingt-neuf*	89

And now you say: $4 \times 20 + 10$ = *quatre-vingt-dix* (90). Now continue with *onze* once again, this time eliminating *et*:

quatre-vingt-onze	91	*quatre-vingt-seize*	96
quatre-vingt-douze	92	*quatre-vingt-dix-sept*	97
quatre-vingt-treize	93	*quatre-vingt-dix-huit*	98
quatre-vingt-quatorze	94	*quatre-vingt-dix-neuf*	99
quatre-vingt-quinze	95		
cent	100	*deux cent un* (No "s")	201
cent un (No "et") [sɑ̃]	101	*trois cents*	300
deux cents	200		

quatre cents, cinq cents, six cents, sept cents, huit cents, neuf cents

mille [mil] 1.000

Note: In **French** a **period** (.) is used to denote **thousands** or **millions**, where in **English** a **comma** (,) is used. Also, a **comma** (,) is used in **French** where **English** uses a **period** (.) for **decimals:** *2,75* (Fr.) = 2.75 (Eng.); *0,55* = .55; *,0426* = .0426, etc.

deux mille (No "s")	2.000
deux mille un	2.001
trois mille	3.000
etc.	
un million [miljɔ̃]	1.000.000
deux millions	2.000.000
etc.	
un milliard [miljar]	1.000.000.000

3.2 Telling Time

Quelle heure est-il? What time is it? *Il est . . .* It is . . .
une heure = 1h = 1:00
une heure cinq = 1h5 = 1:05
une heure dix = 1h10 = 1:10
une heure et quart = 1h15 = 1:15 (*une heure quinze*)
une heure vingt = 1h20 = 1:20
une heure et demie = 1h30 =1:30 (*une heure trente*)

Note: *et* is used only for the **quarter** and **half-hour.**

After the half-hour, you start to **subtract** from the following hour:

deux heures moins vingt-cinq = 1h35 = 1:35
deux heures moins vingt = 1h40 = 1:40 (or twenty-to-two)
deux heures moins le quart = 1h45 = 1:45 (the definite article *le* is
    used only for this measure of time.)
deux heures = 2h = 2:00
midi (cf. mid-day) = 12 noon   *minuit* = 12 p.m.

The French often denote the hours between noon and midnight in military time; this is especially true when referring to the time of appointments, films, concerts, programs, etc. For example, *quatorze heures* (14h) = 2 p.m.; *vingt heures* (20h) = 8 p.m.; etc. Midnight is *vingt-quatre heures.*

Hint: Subtract 12 from the military time to get p.m. time.

3.3 Describing Time

Ways of talking about time:

Quelle est la date aujourd'hui? What's today's date?
Quel jour sommes-nous? What day is it?
C'est le 15 avril. It's April 15.
C'est mardi, le 15 avril. It's Tuesday, April 15.
C'est le 15 aujourd'hui. It's the 15th today.
On est le quinze. It's the 15th.
C'est le quinze avril, mille neuf cent quatre-vingt-quatorze. It's
   April 15, 1994.

3.4 Days of the Week

*Les jours de la semaine: lundi, mardi, mercredi, jeudi, vendredi,
samedi, dimanche.* The days of the week, Monday, Tuesday, etc., are
not capitalized in French.

Note: The French week begins on **Monday,** rather than Sunday.

Hint: Never say *"à" lundi, "en" lundi,* or *"sur" lundi* for **on** Monday; the day of the week alone is sufficient:

*Je verrai Pierre **lundi**.* I'll see Pierre **on Monday.**
*Margo est arrivée **mardi**.* Margo arrived **on Tuesday.**
*Nous allons partir **jeudi**.* We're leaving **on Thursday.**

For the **day in general** use the definite article:

*Elle travaille **le lundi** jusqu'à minuit.* **Mondays** she works until
   midnight.
***Le mercredi,** ils se rencontrent en ville.* They meet in town **on
   Wednesdays.**
*Les enfants n'aiment pas **le dimanche**.* Children don't like **Sun-
   days.**

3.5 Months

The months are very similar to their English cognates but are **not
capitalized:** *janvier, février, mars, avril, mai, juin, juillet, août,
septembre, octobre, novembre, décembre.*

Quel est votre anniversaire? When is your birthday?

C'est le 25 mai. It's May 25.

Je suis né(e) le 13 octobre. I was born on October 13.

Mon anniversaire, c'est le premier août. My birthday is August 1st.

Quelle est la date de la fête nationale américaine? When is America's national holiday?

C'est le 4 juillet. It's July 4th.

Problem Solving Example:

Select the best word in parentheses in the following passage:

> *Le (**quinze, quinz**) (**Septembre, septembre**) est l'anni-versaire de Sophie. C'est un (**vendredi, Vendredi**). Elle va sortir avec ses amis ce soir vers (**sept heures et demie, sept heures et demi**). Sa meilleure amie est toujours en retard. Elle va sortir vers (**huit heures moins vingt, sept heures quarante**).*

*Le **quinze septembre** est l'aniversaire de Sophie. C'est un **vendredi**. Elle va sortir avec ses amis ce soir vers **sept heures et demie**. Sa meilleure amie est toujours en retard. Elle va sortir vers **huit heures moins vingt**.*

Quinze is the correct spelling for "15." Both *septembre* and *vendredi* are correct without capitalization since months and days of the week in French are not capitalized. *Sept heures et demie* is correct because *et demie* agrees with the feminine noun *heures* and is used when speaking of halfhours. *Huit heures moins vingt* is correct because when expressing time in French after the half-hour, you start to subtract from the following hour. For example, 7:40 becomes "twenty- to-eight" (or "eight minus twenty"): *huit heures moins vingt.*

3.6 The Four Seasons: *Les Quatre Saisons*

Le printemps, l'été, l'automne, l'hiver. Spring, summer, autumn (note French spelling change), winter.

In autumn = *en automne; en hiver, en été,* but *au printemps,* because the preposition now precedes a **consonant**.

3.7 Expressing the Year

You may use either form:

1492   *mille quatre cent quatre-vingt-douze* or
         quatorze cent quatre-vingt-douze

1776   *mille sept cent soixante-seize* or
         dix-sept cent soixante-seize

1812   *mille huit cent douze* or
         dix-huit cent douze

1994   *mille neuf cent quatre-vingt-quatorze* or
         dix-neuf cent quatre-vingt-quatorze

2001   *deux mille un*

3.8 Phone Numbers

Quel est votre numéro de téléphone? What's your phone number?

US: (219) 468-9876. *Indicatif régional: deux cent dix-neuf. Quatre cent soixante-huit, quatre-vingt dix-huit, soixante-seize.* Area code: two hundred nineteen. Four hundred sixty-eight, ninety-eight, seventy-six.

French numbers are quoted in four pairs; a typical number in the Paris area is (1) 60.42.27.99. *Composer le un* (Dial 1), *soixante, quarante-deux, vingt-sept, quatre-vingt-dix-neuf.*

3.9 Expressing Age

To talk about **age,** use *"avoir"*:

Quel âge avez-vous? How old are you?

J'ai 23 ans. I'm 23.

Ma sœur a 25 ans et mes parents ont 47 ans. My sister's 25 and my parents are 47.

La France a plus de mille ans. France is more than 1,000 years old.

Problem Solving Example:

 Select the best word in parentheses in the following passage:

> *Jeanne aime mieux (**le hiver, l'hiver**) que (**le été, l'été**).*
> *L'année prochaine, en (**mille neuf cent quatre-vingt dix-**
> ***huit, mille neuf cents quatre vingt dix huit**), elle va faire*
> *du ski. Son grand-père qui (**est, a**) (**soixante-dix-neuf,***
> ***soixante dix neuf**) ans va faire du ski aussi. Quand il*
> *était jeune il était un champion de ski. Son numéro était*
> ***(deux cent un, deux cents et un**).*

 *Jeanne aime mieux **l'hiver** que **l'été**. L'année prochaine,*
> *en **mille neuf cent quatre-vingt-dix-huit**, elle va faire du*
> *ski. Son grand-père qui a **soixante-dix-neuf** ans va faire*
> *du ski aussi. Quand il était jeune il était un champion de*
> *ski. Son numéro était **deux cent un**.*

L'hiver (winter) is correct because the rule states that when final and initial vowels come together, the final vowel is replaced by an apostrophe. Therefore, the "e" in *le* is dropped. *L'été* (summer) is correct since the same rule applies. *Mille neuf cent quatre-vingt-dix-huit* is the correct numeration to use and the double digits are hyphenated. *A* is correct because in French *avoir* is used to express age. *Soixante-dix-neuf* is the correct numeration because the double digits are hyphenated. *Deux cent un* is the correct numeration because there is no "s" and no *et* in *deux cent un* (201).

3.10 Calculations

For **addition, subtraction, multiplication,** and **division:**

2 + 2 = 4	*Deux **plus** deux **font** quatre*
10 – 3 = 7	*Dix **moins** trois **égalent** sept*
20 × 2 = 40	*Vingt **fois** deux **font** quarante*
10 ÷ 5 = 2	*Dix **divisé** par cinq **égalent** deux*

3.11 Comparisons

Comparisons of **equality, inferiority,** and **superiority** are made by using the following structures:

3.11.1 Equality

*Jean a deux sœurs; Pierre a deux sœurs. Jean a **autant de sœurs que** Pierre.* John has two sisters. Pierre has two sisters. John has **as many** sisters as Peter.

*Marie-France gagne 3.000 francs par mois; Simone touche le même salaire. Simone gagne **autant d'argent que** Marie-France.* Marie-France earns 3,000 francs a month; Simone earns the same salary. Simone earns **as much** money as Marie-France.

autant de + noun + ***que*** = comparison of equality: as much as, as many as . . .

3.11.2 Inferiority

*Nous visitons trente villes; vous visitez trente-deux villes. Nous visitons **moins de villes que** vous.* We visit thirty cities; you visit thirty-two cities. We visit **fewer cities than** you.

*Les Duval boivent trois bouteilles de vin mais leurs cousins n'en boivent que deux. Leurs cousins boivent **moins de vin que** les Duval.* The Duvals drink three bottles of wine but their cousins only drink two. Their cousins drink **less wine than** the Duvals.

moins de + noun + ***que*** = less than (singular or plural quantity).

Problem Solving Example:

Correct the following passage by applying numbers and *autant* and *moins*:

> *Marie a une amie à Paris. Son numéro de téléphone est (60) 242-987. Marie gagne autant de l'argent que son amie mais elle voyage moins qu'elle.*

*Marie a une amie à Paris. Son numéro de téléphone est 60.24.29.87. Marie gagne **autant d'argent que** son amie mais elle voyage **moins qu'elle**.*

60.24.29.87 is the way in which telephone numbers are expressed in French. *Autant d'argent que* is used to show how much and the rule states that when final and initial vowels come together, the final vowel is replaced by an apostrophe. *Moins qu'elle* is used to show how little, and the same rule applies concerning final and initial vowels.

3.11.3 Superiority

*Robert a dix-huit livres; tu as quinze livres. Il a **plus de livres que** toi.* Robert has eighteen books; you have fifteen books. He has more books than you.

*Margot passe trois jours à Paris; sa mère y passe cinq jours. Sa mère passe **plus de temps** à Paris **que** Margot.* Margot spends three days in Paris; her mother spends five days. Her mother spends more time in Paris than Margot.

plus de + noun + *que* = more than (singular or plural quantity).

3.11.4 Generalized Comparisons

For comparisons that do not entail numbers but are more **generalized** comparisons, use *autant que, moins que, plus que:*

*Tu lis **autant que** moi.* You read as much as I do.

*Paul parle **moins que** son père.* Paul talks less than his father (does).

*Elisse voyage **plus que** sa sœur.* Elise travels more than her sister.

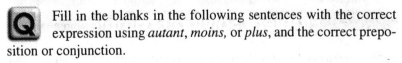

Problem Solving Example:

Q Fill in the blanks in the following sentences with the correct expression using *autant, moins,* or *plus,* and the correct preposition or conjunction.

1. *Mon frère a deux chiens. Ma sœur a deux chiens aussi. Ma sœur a _____ chiens que mon frère.*
2. *Ma sœur est riche mais mon frère et pauvre. Mon frère gagne _____ argent que ma sœur.*

3. *Ma sœur a vu le film dix fois. Mon frère a vu le même film sept fois. Elle a vu le film _____ fois que lui. Les deux adorent le film. Donc, il aime le film _____ elle.*

1. *Mon frère a deux chiens. Ma sœur a deux chiens aussi. Ma sœur a **autant de** chiens que mon frère.*
2. *Ma sœur est riche mais mon frère est pauvre. Mon frère gagne **moins d'**argent que ma sœur.*
3. *Ma sœur a vu le film dix fois. Mon frère a vu le même film sept fois. Elle a vu le film **plus de** fois que lui. Les deux adorent le film. Donc, il aime le film **autant qu'**elle.*

In sentence 1, *autant de* is chosen because it means "as many." In sentence 2, *moins de* is chosen because it means "less." In sentence 3, *plus de* is chosen for the first blank because it means "more." *Autant que* is chosen for the second blank because it means "as much as" and this is a generalized comparison that does not entail specific numbers.

3.12 Ordinal Numbers

To express numbers that represent **consecutive order** (first, tenth, twenty-first, thirtieth, etc.) use:

premier, première	first (m. & f.)
deuxième	second
troisième	third
quatrième	fourth
cinquième	fifth
vingt et unième	twenty-first
etc.	

Note: While the English form of these numbers varies, aside from *premier,* French uses the suffix *"—ième"* for **all numbers.**

Dates are expressed by **cardinal** numbers: *le cinq mai, le vingt-deux septembre, le trente juillet,* even though English uses **ordinal** numbers: the 5th of May, the 22nd of September, July 30th, etc.

Exception: The first day of the month is expressed by the **ordinal** form: *le **premier** juin, le **premier** décembre,* etc.

Problem Solving Example:

Choose the correct word in parentheses:

> *Paul a fini (**deux, deuxième**) dans sa classe. Il va obtenir son diplôme le (**vingt-neuf, vingt-neuvième**) mai. Sa famille va faire une surprise-partie pour lui le (**quatre, quatrième**) juin.*

> *Paul a fini **deuxième** dans sa classe. Il va obtenir son diplôme le **vingt-neuf** mai. Sa famille va faire une surprise-partie pour lui le **quatre** juin.*

Deuxième is used to express consecutive order numbers. *Vingt-neuf* and *quatre* are correct to express dates therefore using cardinal numbers.

Quiz: The Sounds of French – By the Numbers

1. *As-tu demandé _____ Jean . . .*

    (A) *de*   (C) *as*

    (B) *à*   (D) *a*

2. *. . . _____ venir?*

    (A) *a*   (C) *à*

    (B) *des*   (D) *de*

3. *Oui, je lui _____ dit que ellipses*

    (A) *a*   (C) *ai*

    (B) *à*   (D) *as*

4.   . . . *nous l'attendrions* _____.

      (A) *la*   (C) *le*

      (B) *là*   (D) *les*

5.   *Depuis que François a perdu* _____, *il est au chômage.*

      (A) *sa place*   (C) *sa bague*

      (B) *son poste*   (D) *son roman*

6.   *Quelle heure est-il? Il est* _____.

      (A) *deux heures moins-le-quart*

      (B) *deux heures moins-quart*

      (C) *deux heures moins le quart*

      (D) *deux heures moins quart*

7.   *Pour prendre de l'essence, on va a* _____.

      (A) *la station-service*   (C) *l'épicerie*

      (B) *la perfumerie*   (D) *l'essentiel*

8.   *Vingt fois deux* _____ *quarante.*

      (A) *est*   (C) *font*

      (B) *sont*   (D) *fait*

9.   *Arnaud voyage chaque année mais sa sœur ne voyage jamais. Arnaud voyage* _____ *sa sœur.*

      (A) *autant de*   (C) *plus de*

      (B) *autant que*   (D) *plus que*

10. *"Actuellement" veut dire* _____.

    (A) *en réalité*   (C) *maintenant*

    (B) *par une action*   (D) *veritablement*

ANSWER KEY

1.	(B)	6.	(C)
2.	(D)	7.	(A)
3.	(C)	8.	(C)
4.	(B)	9.	(D)
5.	(B)	10.	(C)

CHAPTER 4

Nouns and Articles

4.1 Gender

The gender of French nouns is something that needs to be memorized. There is a trick for guessing the gender of a noun, although it is not a rule and is subject to having exceptions. The rule refers to the ending sounds of words, not the ending letters.

Many masculine nouns end in a consonant sound, e.g., *la salle* [*l*], *la bombe* [*b*]. Many feminine nouns end in a vowel sound, e.g., *le camion* [*ô*], *le chocolat* [*a*].

4.1.1 Masculine Nouns

Nouns which refer to **masculine beings,** both humans and animals:

l'homme, le garçon, le prince, l'empereur, le roi, le duc, le mâle, le cheval, le coq, etc.

Guide to Identifying Masculine Nouns

Ending of Noun	Examples	Exceptions
—age	*l'âge*	*une image*
	le fromage	*une cage*
	le nuage	*la plage*
	un étage	*une page*
	Quel dommage!	

Ending of Noun	Examples	Exceptions
—eur	un professeur le docteur un auteur un ordinateur le bonheur l'extérieur	la faveur une rumeur la chaleur
—isme	le capitalisme le patriotisme le socialisme le féminisme l'impressionnisme	
—ment	l'appartement le département les renseignements un compliment le médicament les vêtements	
Vowels other than [ə]	le cinéma le trou le piano le bureau le café le hibou	la radio l'eau la vertu
Consonant	le raisin le jour le nez le doigt le champ le ciel	la saison l'amour la clef la nuit la mort

Ending of Noun	Examples	Exceptions
Foreign words	*le pique-nique* *le bifteck* *le weekend* *le marketing* *le base-ball* *le parking*	*une interview*

The names of languages are masculine: *le français, le russe, le japonais, l' anglais, l'espangnol, l'italien,* etc.

4.1.2 Feminine Nouns

Nouns that are used to describe **female beings,** both humans and animals:

la femme, une fille, une mère, une tante, la nièce, la reine, la princesse, la poule, la vache, la chatte, la chienne

Guide to Identifying Feminine Nouns

Ending of Noun	Examples	Exceptions
—*ade*	*une promenade* *une tirade* *la limonade*	
—*ance* or —*ence*	*la naissance* *la distance* *l'indépendance* *la différence* *la patience* *la science*	*le silence*
—*oire*	*la gloire* *l'histore* *une poire* *la victoire* *la mémoire*	*le mémoire* – (student paper)

Ending of Noun	Examples	Exceptions
—*sion* or —*tion*	*une impression* *une décision* *la télévision* *la libération* *une condition* *une répétition* *la constitution*	
—*son*	*la saison* *une maison* *la raison* *la liaison* *une chanson*	*le son*
—*é* or —*ée*	*la pensée* *l'idée* *la liberté* *l'égalité* *la bonté*	*le comité*

4.1.3 Feminine Nouns/Masculine Beings

Some **feminine** nouns can refer to **masculine** beings:

*Philippe est **la sentinelle** ce soir.* Philippe is the sentry tonight.

*Georges était **une victime** de l'épidémie.* Georges was a victim of the epidemic.

*Henri est **une personne** importante.* Henri is an important person.

4.1.4 Masculine Nouns/Feminine Beings

Some **masculine** nouns can refer to **feminine** beings:

*Elle est **écrivain**.* She's a writer. (or) *C'est une femme **écrivain**.*

***Mon professeur** est une femme intelligente.* My professor is an intelligent woman.

4.1.5 Identical Forms/Different Meanings

Some nouns have identical masculine and feminine forms but different meanings:

Masculine		Feminine	
un livre	a book	*une livre*	a pound
un page	a page-boy	*une page*	a page
un tour	a turn	*une tour*	a tower
un vase	a vase	*la vase*	mud or sludge
le critique	the critic	*la critique*	criticism

4.2 Formation of Feminine Nouns

Many feminine nouns are formed by adding "e" to the masculine:

l'ami/l'amie, le cousin/la cousine, un voisin/une voisine, le bergèr/ la bergère, l'étudiant/l'étudiante

However, some feminine nouns can be formed by substituting the masculine ending —*eur* with —*euse* or —*rice*.

—*eur* to —*euse*	to —*rice*
le vendeur / la vendeuse	*l'acteur / l'actrice*
le danser / la danseuse	*le directeur / la directrice*
le menteur / la menteuse	*le lecteur / la lectrice*
le coiffeur / la coiffeuse	*le tuteur / la tutrice*

4.2.1 Variant Forms

Some feminine nouns are quite different from their masculine counterparts:

Masculine	Feminine
le père	*la mère*
le frère	*la sœur*
l'homme	*la femme* (woman)
le mari	*la femme* (wife)
un dieu	*une déesse*

le roi	*la reine*
un neveu	*une nièce*
un oncle	*une tante*
un héros	*une héroïne*
le gendre	*la bru*
un coq	*une poule*
un cerf	*une biche*

4.2.2 Same Form for Masculine and Feminine

Some nouns use the same form for describing both male and female:

un/une enfant; un/une artiste; un/une camarade; un/une esclave; un/une philosophe; un/une secrétaire, etc.

Problem Solving Example:

Select the best word in parentheses in the following passage:

> *Cette femme s'appelle Patricia. Elle est (**secrétaire**, **secretairée**), mais elle aime danser et voudrait devenir (**danseur**, **danseuse**) ou bien (**acteur**, **actrice**) un jour. Son mari est (**artist**, **artiste**). Patricia et son mari veulent avoir deux (**enfants**, **enfantes**). La sœur de Patricia a deux enfants, un garçon et une fille. Son neveu s'appelle Jean et sa (**neveuse**, **nièce**) s'appelle Hélène.*

> *Cette femme s'appelle Patricia. Elle est **secrétaire**, mais elle aime danser et voudrait devenir **danseuse** ou bien **actrice** un jour. Son mari est **artiste**. Patricia et son mari veulent avoir deux **enfants**. La sœur de Patricia a deux enfants, un garçon et une fille. Son neveu s'appelle Jean et sa **nièce** s'appelle Hélène.*

Secrétaire is correct because there is only one form of this word to describe both male and female. *Danseuse* and *actrice* are correct because Patricia is female and both words have female variations of the male forms of the words. *Artiste* is correct because there is only one form of this word to describe both male and female. *Enfant* has only one form as well, so *enfants* is the only correct answer. *Nièce* is the correct choice because it is one of the feminine nouns that are completely different from their male counterparts.

4.3   Plural Nouns

Normally, as in English, the plural of nouns is formed by adding an "s" to the singular:

le stylo/les stylos; la table/les tables; l'arbre/les arbres; l'ami/les amis, and *l'amie/les amies,* etc.

4.3.1   Nouns Ending in "s," "x," or "z"

Nouns that end in "s," "x," or "z" do not add "s" for the plural:

le repas/les repas; la croix/les croix; le nez/les nez

4.3.2   Some Irregular Plural Nouns

Singular Ending	Plural	Exceptions
—al, —ail:		
journal	*journaux*	*bals*
animal	*animaux*	*récitals*
cheval	*chevaux*	*carnavals*
canal	*canaux*	*festivals*
métal	*métaux*	*chacals*
mal	*maux*	
vitrail	*vitraux*	*chandails*
travail	*travaux*	*détails*
—au, —eu, —eau:		
noyau	*noyaux*	*pneus*
eau	*eaux*	
neveu	*neveux*	
niveau	*niveaux*	

—*ou:* Most take "s" in the plural		**7 exceptions:**
fou	*fous*	*bijoux*
cou	*cous*	*cailloux*
sou	*sous*	*choux*
trou	*trous*	*genoux*
		hiboux
		joujoux
		poux

4.3.3 Three Plural Nouns That Are Very Irregular

un œil / des yeux – an eye / eyes

le ciel / les cieux – sky, as in weather / Heaven

le jeune homme / les jeunes gens – young man / young folks

Note: *ciels* is also used in poetry and in discussing paintings; e.g., *les ciels de Gauguin.*

4.3.4 Three Feminine Nouns That Are Always Plural

les mathématiques (often shortened to *les maths*)

les vacances

les fiançailles

4.3.5 Family Names

Family names do not change in the plural form except for those of royal dynasties:

la famille Duval, les Duval – the Duvals; *la famille Mitterrand, les Mitterrand* – the Mitterrands

but:

les Bourbons, les Plantagenêts

4.3.6 Plural of Compound Nouns

Some compound nouns contain verbs and adverbs that are invariable. Nouns and adjectives are sometimes pluralized.

Singular	Plural
un gratte-ciel	*des gratte-ciel*
	("sky" is singular)
une pomme de terre	*des pommes de terre*
	("earth" is singular)
un coffre-fort	*des coffres-forts*
un arc-en-ciel	*des arcs-en-ciel*
un chef-d'œuvre	*des chefs-d'œuvre*

Check the dictionary to be sure of the correct plural form of compound nouns.

Problem Solving Example:

Using the cues given in bold, fill in the blanks with the appropriate singular or plural forms of the nouns.

1. *J'ai un **stylo**, et mon amie Martine a trois _____.*
2. *Un cyclope n'a qu'un seul _____; mais les humains ont deux **yeux**.*
3. *Je reçois le **journal** Libération. Mes parents reçoivent trois _____.*
4. *Le **vitrail** à Notre-Dame est très beau. Je fais une étude sur les _____.*
5. *Mon père a un **neveu** et mon grand-père a dix _____.*
6. *J'ai acheté un _____ pour cette recette, mais il me faut deux **choux**!*
7. *Les **poux** sont dégoûtants! Regardez! J'ai attrapé un _____.*
8. *Il y a un **gratte-ciel**; il y a dix _____ dans le centre de la ville.*

1. *stylos*
2. *œil*
3. *journaux*
4. *vitraux*
5. *neveux*
6. *chou*

7. *pou*
8. *gratte-ciel*

4.4   The Article

The article introduces the noun and may be definite or indefinite. **It is usually repeated before each noun.** Although in English we often omit articles, in French **the noun must always** be preceded by an article.

4.4.1   Definite Articles: "The"

	Masculine	Feminine
Singular	*le* garçon	*la* femme
	le billet	*la* maison
	le soir	*la* plage
Plural	*les* garçons	*les* femmes
	les billets	*les* maisons
	les soirs	*les* plages

Note: When a singular noun begins with a vowel, the article becomes *l'*:

	Masculine	Feminine
	*l'*ami	*l'*amie
	*l'*aéroport	*l'*école
	*l'*œil	*l'*usine

4.4.2   Repetition of the Article

Articles are generally repeated before each noun in a series:

J'ai invité tout le monde: la mère, le fils, la fille, l'oncle et les cousins. I invited everyone: the mother, son, daughter, uncle, and cousins.

4.4.3   Contractions with an Article

After the prepositions *à* and *de* (at the, to the, in the, of the, from the), some forms of the definite article contract:

$$à + la = à \ la$$
$$à + le = \underline{au}$$
$$à + l' = à \ l'$$
$$à + les = \underline{aux}$$

Nous sommes allés à l'ecole. We went to the school.

Nous avons parlé à la secrétaire. We spoke to the secretary.

***Au** début de la semaine, il écrira **aux** clients.* At the beginning of the week, he'll write to the customers.

*Il fera beau **au** printemps.* It will be nice weather in the spring.

$$de + la = de \ la$$
$$de + le = \underline{du}$$
$$de + l' = de \ l'$$
$$de + les = \underline{des}$$

*Jean est le père **de l'**enfant.* Jean is the father of the child.

*As-tu appris les paroles **de la** chanson?* Did you learn the words to the song?

*C'est le plus beau pays **du** monde, le pays **des** merveilles.* It's the most beautiful country in the world, the land of marvels.

*Ils reviennent **du** sud.* They're returning from the south.

Problem Solving Example:

 Combine the two thoughts given in order to create a sentence, making sure to use proper proposition-article contractions when necessary.

1. *la bière; J'ai bu de . . .*
2. *le pain; Avez-vous de . . .?*
3. *l'école; Je vais à . . .*
4. *les épinards; Mme Renaud parle toujours de . . .*
5. *le prof; As-tu encore parlé à . . .*
6. *le vin; Il a déjà commandé de . . .*
7. *les jolies filles; Les garçons de notre lycée ne parlent guère à . . .*
8. *l'eau; Il m'a dit qu'il veut de . . .*

1. *J'a bu **de la** bière.*
2. *Avez-vous **du** pain?*
3. *Je vais à l'école.*
4. *Mme Renaud parle toujours **des** épinards.*
5. *As-tu encore parlé **au** prof?*
6. *Il a déjà commandé **du** vin.*
7. *Les garçons de notre lycée ne parlent guère **aux** jolies filles.*
8. *Il m'a dit qu'il veut **de l'eau.***

4.5 Special Uses of the Definite Article

The definite article is used to make generalized observations:

Les voitures de sport sont chères. Sports cars are expensive.

Les oiseaux mangent tout le temps. Birds eat constantly.

Note: In English we often omit the article in these kinds of statements.

4.5.1 The Definite Article with *Aimer, Préférer, Adorer, Détester*

An easy acronym is "A PAD."

Since these four verbs express one's **general** feeling about a person, place or thing, they **always** take the definite article.

*Nous **aimons les films** français.* We like French films.

*Laure **adore la vanille** mais elle **déteste le chocolat.*** Laure loves vanilla but hates chocolate.

*Préfères-tu **le bleu** ou **le rouge?*** Do you prefer blue or red?

4.5.2 With Titles, Professions, and Countries

The definite article is used when addressing or describing titled or important individuals:

Titles:

le président, la comtesse, le sénateur, etc.

*Oui, monsieur **le Président. Le Président** Mitterrand a parlé.* Yes, Mr. President. President Mitterrand spoke.

Professions:

Le docteur Duval est arrivé. Doctor Duval has arrived.

Countries: "Feminine" countries (i.e., those whose final letter is *"e"*) are preceded by the definite article when they are the **subject** or **direct object** of the verb:

La France est belle. France is beautiful.

J'ai visité l'Italie et la Belgique. I visited Italy and Belgium.

Use *le* for **"masculine" countries** (those which end in a consonant):

Le Japon exporte beaucoup de produits électroniques. Japan exports a lot of electronic products.

Elles vont visiter le Danemark et le Brésil. They will visit Denmark and Brazil.

Exceptions:

1. *Le Mexique.* Mexico.

2. No article is used when discussing islands: *Tahiti est très beau.* Tahiti is very beautiful.

3. No article is used before Israel: *Ils connaissent bien Israël.* They know Israel well.

Les is used for plural countries:

Les Etats-Unis. The United States.

Les Pays-Bas. The Netherlands.

4.6 The Indefinite Article

The indefinite articles "a," "an," "some," "any" are used to refer to a non-specific noun.

Masculine	Feminine	Plural
un livre	*une lettre*	*des cousins*
un stylo	*une jupe*	*des lunettes*
un jardin	*une chanson*	*des bonbons*

Ils ont acheté des légumes. They bought some vegetables.

Jacques a reçu une lettre. Jack received a letter.

C'est un bon livre. It's a good book.

4.6.1 Special Uses of the Indefinite Article

Use the indefinite article to answer a question:

Qu'est-ce que c'est? What is it? (or "this")?

C'est une discussion importante. It's an important discussion.

Qui est-ce? Who is it? (or "this")?

C'est une bonne amie. She's a good friend.

Also use the indefinite article to describe a profession, or a religious or political persuasion:

Voilà Pierre. C'est un médecin célèbre. There's Pierre. He's a famous doctor.

Mme Aumont, c'est une catholique orthodoxe. Mrs. Aumont is a devout Catholic.

Remember the rule: *C'est un, une, le, la* + noun **for identification.** *Ce sont* + *les* or *des* may be used for plural nouns.

Problem Solving Example:

Fill in the blanks with the correct usage of definite and indefinite articles:

> *Jean attend _____ vacances. Il va aller _____ Japon. Il voudrait visiter _____ Mexique aussi mais il n'a pas le temps. Son frère aime voyager aussi. Il adore _____ plage. Il va visiter _____ Brésil _____ Tahiti. Je vais acheter _____ livre pour Jean parce que je veux lui donner un cadeau avant son voyage.*

A *Jean attend **les** vacances. Il va aller **au** Japon. Il voudrait visiter **le** Mexique aussi mais il n'a pas le temps. Son frère aime voyager aussi. Il adore **la** plage. Il va visiter **le** Brésil **ou** Tahiti. Je vais acheter **un** livre pour Jean parce que je veux lui donner un cadeau avant son voyage.*

Les is used in front of *vacances* because *vacances* is plural. *Au* is the contraction of *à* and *le*, and *Japon* is a masculine country because it ends in a consonant. *Mexique* is an exception to this rule, so *le* is used. *La* is correct because *adorer* is used and the rule states that when a verb expresses one's general feelings about a thing, it always takes the definite article. *Le* precedes *Brésil* because it is a masculine country ending in a consonant. Nothing precedes *Tahiti* because no article is used when discussing islands. *Un* is correct for the last blank because no other book was mentioned, as using *le* would imply, and *livre* is masculine.

CHAPTER 5

The Partitive Article

(Le Partitif)

5.1 General Use

The partitive is based on describing **"a part** of all the . . . that exists in the world." While in English, "some" or "any" may be omitted, the partitive article must be expressed in French, except in certain structures.

5.2 Formation

		Partitive	Example
Masculine	*de + le*	*du*	*Voulez-vous **du** vin?* Do you want some/any wine?
	de + l'	*de l'*	*As-tu **de** l'argent?* Do you have any money?
Feminine	*de + la*	*de la*	*Elle a acheté **de la** crème.* She bought some cream.
	de + l'	*de l'*	*J'ai soif et je voudrais de l'eau.* I'm thirsty and I would like some water.

		Partitive	Example
Plural	*de + les*	*des*	*Nous cherchons **des** livres intéressants.* We're looking for some interesting books. *Margot a acheté **des** robes chic.* Margot bought some chic dresses.

5.3 Omission of the Definite Article after "de"

Although the partitive article must always be expressed to mean "some" or "any," there are certain exceptions to this rule in which the partitive is omitted.

5.3.1 With Negative Expressions

In negative expressions such as *pas de*, *plus de* and *jamais de*, the partitive is omitted and only *de* is used.

pas de   *Simone n'a **pas d'**amis.* Simon doesn't have any friends.

plus de   *Nous ne voulons **plus de** problèmes.* We don't want any more problems.

jamais de   *Il ne porte **jamais de** cravate.* He never wears a tie.

5.3.2 Before a Plural Noun Preceded by an Adjective

In cases when the noun that the partitive article reflects has an adjective before it, the partitive article is omitted and only "*de*" is used.

*Nous avons vu **de belles maisons**.* We saw some beautiful homes.

*Nous avons vu **des maisons blanches**.* We saw some white houses.

*Ce chien a **de grands yeux**.* This dog has big eyes.

*Ce chien a **des yeux intéressants**.* This dog has interesting eyes.

5.3.3 With Adverbs of Quantity

Adverbs that describe quantity use only *de* before a noun.

beaucoup de	*Elle a eu **beaucoup de** chance.* She had lots of luck.
trop de	*Manges-tu **trop de** pain?* Do you eat too much bread?
assez de	*Il n'avait pas **assez d'**argent pour le billet.* He didn't have enough money for the ticket.
un peu de/peu de	*Nous voulons **un peu de** soupe et peu de viande.* We want a little soup and not much meat.

5.3.4 After Certain Expressions

There are certain expressions that call for the omission of the definite article before a noun.

avoir besoin de	*J'ai besoin de vacances.* I need a vacation.
avoir envie de	*As-tu envie de gâteau?* Do you feel like having some cake?

5.4 Definite, Indefinite, or Partitive Article

5.4.1 The Definite Article

The definite article **describes a specific noun:**

*Nous avons visité **le musée, la tour,** et **les vieux bâtiments**.* We visited the museum, the tower, and the old buildings.

The definite article **makes a general observation:**

***Les vitamines** sont bonnes pour **la santé**.* Vitamins are good for your health.

5.4.2 Indefinite Article

The indefinite article refers to a class of persons or things that are **not specifically identified:**

***Un homme** lui a parlé.* A man spoke to her.

*Nous avons lu **une histoire** triste.* We read a sad story.

*Y a-t-il **des chats** chez toi?* Are there (any) cats at your house?

5.4.3 The Partitive Article

The partitive article describes quantities that are **a part of an entire class of people or objects:**

*Nous avons rencontré **des gens intéressants**.* We met (some) interesting people.

*Il n'a pas lu beaucoup **d'articles**.* He didn't read many articles.

*Nos invités prennent **du thé** le matin.* Our guests drink tea in the morning.

5.4.4 Résumé

*--Voulez-vous **de l'eau**?*

*--Non, merci, je ne veux **pas d'eau** parce que je n'aime pas l'eau. Je préfère **le coca**.*

*--Mais **l'eau** ici est spéciale. Prenez seulement **un peu d'eau** et vous verrez.*

*--D'accord. Mais ne me donnez qu'**un petit verre d'eau** et nous resterons **de bons amis**.*

"Do you want some water?"

"No, thanks, I don't want any water because I don't like water. I prefer Coke."

"But the water here is special. Have just a bit of water and you'll see."

"All right. But give me only a small glassful and we'll remain good friends."

Problem Solving Example:

Fill in the blanks correctly using *de, du,* and *des*:

Carole va au supermarché pour acheter _____ légumes et _____ fromage. Elle voudrait aller à la librairie aussi pour acheter _____ bons livres parce qu'elle lit beaucoup _____ romans. Mais elle ne peut pas aller à la librairie parce qu'elle n'a pas beaucoup _____ argent. Le lendemain soir elle va au restaurant avec son amie. Elle voudrait _____ café mais elle prend _____ eau parce qu'elle ne prend pas _____ café le soir.

*Carole va au supermarché pour acheter **des** légumes et **du** fromage. Elle voudrait aller à la librairie aussi pour acheter **de bons livres** parce qu'elle lit beaucoup de romans. Mais elle ne peut pas aller à la librairie parce qu'elle n'a pas beaucoup d'argent. Len demain soir, elle va au restaurant avec son amie. Elle voudrait **du** café mais elle prend **de l'**eau parce qu'elle ne prend pas de café le soir.*

Des is the partitive article used before *légumes*. *Du* is the partitive article used before *fromage*. The partitive is needed in both cases because Carole is only going to buy some of the *légumes* and *fromage* in the store. They represent part of all the *légumes* and *fromage* available at the store. *De* is correct because there is a plural adjective that precedes the noun so the partitive is omitted. *De* is correct again because it is used with the adverb of quantity *beaucoup*. *D'argent* is correct because *beaucoup* is an adverb of quantity. *Du* is the right answer because there is a masculine noun *café* that calls for a partitive article *le* which combines with *de* to form *du*. *De l'eau* is correct because there must be a partitive to signify "some" water. *De* is correct in the last blank because when there is a negative expression, the partitive article must be omitted.

Quiz: Nouns and Articles & The Partitive Article

1. *À la fin du repas j'aime prendre _____ .*

   (A) *de café*   (C) *du café*

   (B) *de la café*   (D) *de la café*

2. *Je veux ouvrir cette porte. Où est _____ clef?*

   (A) *un*   (C) *le*

   (B) *une*   (D) *la*

3. *J'adore le Rouge et le noir, mais _____ critique n'aime pas _____ livre.*

   (A) *la, ce*   (C) *le, ce*

   (B) *le, cette*   (D) *la, cette*

4. *À la pharmacie Margot a acheté _____ .*

   (A) *de médicaments*   (C) *les médicaments*

   (B) *des médicaments*   (D) *du médicament*

5. *Madame Rosemonde est _____ d'histoire.*

   (A) *ma professeur*   (C) *ma professeure*

   (B) *mon professeur*   (D) *mon professeure*

6. *Les _____ de la reine sont rares.*

   (A) *bijou*   (C) *bijoux*

   (B) *bijous*   (D) *bijoutiers*

7. *Qu'est que vous allez faire pendant* _____ ?

    (A) *les grands vacances* (C) *le grand vacance*

    (B) *les grandes vacances* (D) *la grande vacance*

8. *Ce matin, pour le petit déjeuner, j'ai mangé* _____ .

    (A) *les pommes de terre* (C) *des pommes de terre*

    (B) *les pommes de terres* (D) *des pommes des terres*

9. *Je me rapelle de ces jours délicieux que j'ai passés dans ce petit village avec Ursule. Oui, j'en garde* _____ .

    (A) *le mémoire*   (C) *des beaux souvenirs*

    (B) *un mémoire*   (D) *de beaux souvenirs*

10. *Mes cousins veulent visiter* _____ *un jour.*

    (A) *L'Isreäl*   (C) *le Danemark*

    (B) *la Mexique*   (D) *le Belgique*

ANSWER KEY

1.	(C)	6.	(C)
2.	(D)	7.	(B)
3.	(C)	8.	(C)
4.	(B)	9.	(D)
5.	(B)	10.	(C)

CHAPTER 6

Adjectives

6.1 Function

Adjectives **qualify** or **describe** nouns and pronouns and may be either concrete or abstract in meaning.

*C'est une **grande** maison.* It's a large house.

*C'est un examen **important**.* It's an important exam.

6.1.1 Agreement in Gender and Number

Adjectives vary in **number** and **gender** to **agree** with the nouns they modify.

***Philippe** est **blond** et ses **sœurs** sont **blondes** aussi.* Philippe is blonde and his sisters are blonde too.

*La **vieille église** se trouve à côté d'un **vieux château**.* The old church is situated near an old castle.

*Elle porte **des bas blancs** et **des souliers noirs**.* She's wearing white stockings and black shoes.

6.2 Formation of Feminine

With regular adjectives, add an "e" to the masculine to make the feminine form:

petit/petite; rond/ronde; fort/forte

Adjectives that end in "e" are invariable:

une rue large; un stylo rouge; un/une autre enfant

Chic is also invariable; as are *génial, saper,* and *extra*

un hôtel chic; une robe chic

6.2.1 Common Irregular Forms

There are several irregular feminine adjectives that are not formed by adding an "e" to the masculine form.

Masculine	Feminine
un mur épais	*une tête épaisse*
un faux ami	*une fausse amie*
un esprit vif	*une couleur vive*
un air doux	*une chanson douce*
un garçon malin	*une fille maligne*
un stylo favori	*une robe favorite*
un vin sec	*une peau sèche*
un homme sérieux	*une femme sérieuse*
de l'air frais	*une idée fraîche*

The plural form of these irregular adjectives agrees in gender with the subject it modifies.

des esprits vifs	uses the regular masculine form of the adjective because *esprit* is masculine.
des choses favorites	uses the irregular feminine form of the adjective because *chose* is feminine.

6.3 Position of Adjectives

The majority of adjectives **follow** the noun:

un vin blanc

une maison blanche

However, there are about a dozen adjectives that **precede** the nouns they modify. They include:

Masculine	Feminine
un **autre** cheval	une **autre** personne
un **beau*** garçon	une **belle** fille
un **bon** livre	une **bonne** histoire
un **certain** homme	une **certaine** femme
un **grand** problème	une **grande** montagne
un **gros** nez	une **grosse** poule
un **jeune** enfant	une **jeune** enfant
un **joli** chapeau	une **jolie** robe
un **long** chemin	une **longue** leçon
un **mauvais** jour	une **mauvaise** vie
un **nouveau*** complet	une **nouvelle** situation
un **vieux*** soldat	une **vieille** dame

* Each of these three adjectives has another form used before **masculine nouns with initial vowels or h:**

	beau	*nouveau*	*vieux*
Singular	*bel*	*nouvel*	*vieil*
Plural	*beaux*	*nouveaux*	*vieux*

un bel arbre – a beautiful tree
de beaux arbres – beautiful trees
un nouvel endroit – a new place
de nouveaux endroits – new places
un vieil état – an old state
de vieux états – old states
un vieil homme – an old man

Remember that the correct form of the plural is *de grandes montagnes* and *de jolis chapeaux* because when a plural adjective precedes a noun the partitive article is omitted.

6.3.1 Before or After a Noun with the Same Meaning

Many adjectives may be placed before or after the noun for stylistic effect, **without a change in meaning:**

Joyeux Noël/un Noël joyeux; une merveilleuse surprise/une surprise merveilleuse

6.3.2 Change in Position, Change in Meaning

Some adjectives may change meaning with a change in position:

un pauvre enfant – a poor child
un enfant pauvre – a child without money

un professeur ancien – an aged teacher
un ancien professeur – a former teacher

une brave personne – a good person (in character)
une personne brave – a courageous person

mon cher oncle – my dear uncle
ma voiture chère – my expensive car

un grand homme – a great man (famous, important)
un homme grand – a tall man

le même jour – the same day
le jour même – the very day

> *Nous arrivons **le même jour** que toi.* We're arriving the same day as you are.
> *Il est parti **le jour même** de son mariage.* He left on the very day of his wedding.

le mois dernier – last month (compared to this month)
le dernier mois – the last month (in a series)

> *Décembre est **le dernier mois** de l'année.* December is the last month of the year.

propre – showing possession
propre – clean

> *Elle utilise **sa propre voiture**.* She uses her own car.

*Cette **maison propre** est admirable.* This clean house is admirable.

certain – a vague number
certain – sure

Certaines *gens* sont impolis.* Some people are impolite.
*Son voyage est **certain**.* His trip is a sure thing.

* Note: *Gens* is **feminine** when it has an adjective **preceding** it and **masculine** when it has an adjective **following** it: *de **bonnes gens;** des **gens heureux.***

6.3.3 Adjectives of Color

Most adjectives of color are placed after the noun and form the feminine by adding "e":

vert/verte; gris/grise; noir/noire

Note these exceptions:

*un ciel **bleu***	*une cravate **bleue***	*des livres **bleus***
*un chien **blanc***	*une chemise **blanche***	
*un ruban **violet***	*une veste **violette***	
*un crayon **marron***	*une table **marron****	*des cheveux **marron***

*Note: *Marron* (chestnut brown) is a noun and therefore is invariable.

*un chapeau **bleu marine***   *une robe **bleu marine*** (navy blue)
*un papier **rose foncé**** (deep pink)   *une robe **rose clair**** (light pink)

*Note: *Clair, foncé* and compound colors are invariable.

Problem Solving Example:

Q Choose the correct adjective form from the choices in parentheses.

*Le (**vieux, vieil**) homme marchait lentement dans le (**joli jardin, jardin joli**). Dans le jardin il y avait un (**bel, beau**) arbre et des fleurs (**blancs, blanches**). L'homme a mangé un sandwich à côté d'un (**monument ancien, ancien monument**).*

> *Le **vieil** homme marchait lentement dans le **joli jardin**.*
> *Dans le jardin il y avait un **bel** arbre et des fleurs **blanches**.*
> *L'homme a mangé un sandwich à côté d'un **monument**
> **ancien**.*

Vieil is correct because *vieux* has a special form to use in front of a masculine noun that begins with vowel or an "h." *Joli jardin* is correct because *joli* is one of the adjectives that precedes the noun that it modifies. *Bel* is correct because *beau* has a special form to use in front of a masculine noun that begins with a vowel or an "h." *Blanches* is correct because *fleur* is a feminine noun. *Monument ancien* is correct because when *ancien* follows a noun it means "aged" or "ancient" (in this case, "the old monument"). When it precedes a noun, *ancien* means "former."

6.4 Comparing with Adjectives

For comparisons of **equality,** use *aussi* + adjective + *que:*

*Françoise est **aussi intelligente que** son frère.* Françoise is as smart as her brother.

*Jeannette est **aussi jolie que** sa sœur.* Jeannette is as pretty as her sister.

*Un chien est **aussi amusant qu'**un chat.* A dog is as much fun as a cat.

6.4.1 Superiority and Inferiority

For comparisons of **superiority** and **inferiority,** use regular adjectives and add *plus* or *moins*:

*Ce livre est **plus cher** que l'autre.* This book is more expensive than the other.

*Sa veste est **plus longue** que la mienne.* His jacket is longer than mine.

*As-tu un **plus petit morceau** de gâteau?* Do you have a smaller piece of cake?

*Elle cherche une **plus jolie maison** qui est **moins chère.*** She is looking for a nicer house that's cheaper.

Problem Solving Example:

 Based on the information given in each pair of sentences, write a sentence using the comparative.

1. *René parle un peu. Charles parle beaucoup.*
2. *Mon père mange souvent. Je ne mange pas souvent.*
3. *J'ai mangé trois pommes. J'ai mangé deux oranges.*
4. *Je parle tout le temps. Michel parle tout le temps.*
5. *J'ai 25 ans. Mon frère a 23 ans.*

1. *René parle **moins que** Charles.* **OR** *Charles parle **plus que René.***
2. *Mon père mange **plus souvent que** moi.* **OR** *Je mange **moins souvent que mon père.***
3. *J'ai mangé **plus de** pommes **que** d'oranges.* **OR** *J'ai mangé **moins d'oranges que de** pommes.*
4. *Je parle **autant que** Michel.* **OR** *Michel parle **autant que** moi.*
5. *Je suis **plus** âgé **que** mon frère.* **OR** *Mon frère est **moins** âgé **que** moi.*

6.4.2   *Bon/Meilleur*

The comparative of *bon* is *meilleur* and of *bonne* is *meilleure.*

Just as you don't say "gooder" in English, you don't say it in French!

*Ce **vin** est **meilleur** que le vin suédois.* This wine is better than Swedish wine.

*Je voudrais acheter **une meilleure télévision.*** I'd like to buy a better television.

For a **negative** comparison of *bon:*

*Celui-ci est un mauvais restaurant mais Chez Jean est **pire*** (or ***plus mauvais**).* This [one] is a bad restaurant but Chez Jean is worse. (You can also use ***moins bon**.*)

The **negative** comparative of *bon* is *pire*, which means "worse."

(You can also use *plus mauvais*, which means "more bad," or *moins bon*, which means "less good," to make a negative comparison.)

6.4.3 Petit/Moindre

Petit has an irregular form when used in an abstract sense:

Cette loi est de moindre importance. This law is of less importance.

When used in a concrete sense:

Leur bateau est plus petit que le nôtre. Their boat is smaller than ours.

6.4.4 Superlatives

Just as in English, the superlative is formed by **adding the definite article to the comparative.**

For adjectives that precede the noun: *le plus, le moins* + adjective + *de* + noun (the most, the least . . . in the . . .)

Il a acheté la plus belle voiture du village. He bought the most beautiful car in the village.

La plus petite fille de l'école va chanter. The smallest girl in the school is going to sing.

Voilà le moins bon vin de la saison. There's the worst wine of the season.

Il choisit les meilleurs desserts pour la fête. He's choosing the best desserts for the party.

Adjectives that follow the noun: The superlative is formed by **naming the noun** and **adding the article and the adjective.** Note that there are **two definite articles** in this structure.

Nous avons vu le film le plus populaire de l'année. We saw the most popular film of the year.

Qui est l'étudiant le moins intelligent du lycée? Who is the least intelligent student in the high school?

J'ai rencontré la femme la plus célèbre de Washington. I met the most famous woman in Washington.

Problem Solving Example:

 Rewrite each of the following sentences by using the super-lative

1. *C'est un cours intéressant.*
2. *M. Marchand est un professeur intelligent.*
3. *C'est un grand livre.*
4. *C'est une bonne chanson.*
5. *Ce sont de beaux garçons.*

 1. *C'est le cours **le plus intéressant**.*
2. *M. Marchand est le professeur **le plus intelligent**.*
3. *C'est **le plus grand** livre.*
4. *C'est **la meilleure** chanson.*
5. *Ce sont **les plus beaux** garçons.*

6.5 Possessive Adjectives

Since all adjectives **agree with the nouns they modify,** possessive adjectives also follow this rule. Unlike English, where the **possessor** determines the number and gender (his car, her uncles), in French the **object possessed** determines the adjective's gender and number.

6.5.1 Masculine

Masculine singular: one owner, one object

mon livre	my book
ton ami	your friend (**You** can be male or female; the **friend** is male.)
son oncle	his or her uncle (Gender of the **possessor** is determined by the **context.**)

Masculine plural: one owner, two or more objects

mes livres	my books
tes amis	your friends
ses oncles	his or her uncles

6.5.2 Feminine

Feminine singular:

ma robe	my dress
ta cousine	your cousin (**You** can be male or female; the cousin is female.)
sa maison	his or her house

Feminine plural:

mes robes	my dresses
tes cousines	your female cousins
ses maisons	his or her houses

6.5.3 Plural Owners

Plural owners: one masculine or feminine object

notre père – our father
votre mère – your mother
leur jardin – their garden

Plural owners: two or more masculine or feminine objects

nos voitures – our cars
vos parents – your parents
leurs bateaux – their boats

6.5.4 *Mon, Ton,* and *Son* before a Feminine Noun

Always use *mon, ton,* and *son* before a feminine noun that begins with a vowel. However, if there is an adjective that precedes the feminine noun beginning with a vowel, use the regular feminine forms *ma, ta,* and *sa.*

Feminine Nouns Beginning with a Vowel	Feminine Nouns Beginning with a Vowel That have Preceding Adjectives
*Voilà **mon** amie Lara.*	*Voilà **ma bonne** amie Lara.*
There's my friend Lara.	Here is my good friend Lara.
*Elle a oublié **ton** adresse.*	*Elle a oublié pas **ta nouvelle** adresse.*

She forgot your address.   She doesn't know your new address.

Son enfant *est malade.*   **Sa petite enfant** *est malade.*

Her child is sick.   Her small child is sick.

Problem Solving Example:

Fill in the blanks of the following paragraph with the proper possessive adjectives.

Chère Michèle,

Dans cette lettre, _____ amie, je vais te parler de _____ famille. Nous sommes très sportifs. Moi, je fait du judo, mon frère Paul fait du foot, et ma sœur Catherine aime danser. Mon frère Charles est le plus jeune de la famille et il s'amuse avec _____ voisins. Paul a une petite amie aussi. Elle s'appelle Mirabelle. Mirabelle est très sympa et elle est _____ bonne amie.

Pour les vacances de Noël, nous irons chez _____ grands-parents. Ils habitent dans le sud du la France. Eh bien, qu'est-ce que tu fais pendant _____ vacances de Noël?

Maman m'a dit que je dois me remettre au travail. Je dois étudier _____ leçon sur les États-Unis. À bientôt!

Amitiés,
Martine

Chère Michèle,

*Dans cette lettre, **mon** amie, je vais te parler de **ma** famille. Nous sommes très sportifs. Moi, je fait du judo, mon frère Paul fait du foot, et ma sœur Catherine aime danser. Mon frère Charles est le plus jeune de la famille et il s'amuse avec **nos** voisins. Paul a une petite amie aussi. Elle s'appelle Mirabelle. Mirabelle est très sympa et elle est **ma** bonne amie.*

*Pour les vacances de Noël, nous irons chez **nos/mes** grand-parents. Ils habitent dans le sud de la France. Eh ben, qu'est-ce que tu fais pendant **tes** vacances de Noël?*

*Maman m'a dit que je dois me remettre au travail. Je dois étudier **ma** leçon sur les États-Unis. À bientôt!*

Amitiés,
Martine

Mon is the correct choice for the first blank. Although *amie* is feminine, before a feminine noun that begins with a vowel a masculine possessive adjective is used. *Ma* is correct because it reflects the singular feminine noun *famille*. *Nos* is the correct answer because the possessive reflects the plural noun *voisins*. *Ma* is correct this time because when a feminine noun beginning with a vowel is preceded by an adjective, a feminine possessive adjective is used. Both *nos* and *mes* are correct because both reflect the plural noun *grandparents* and our grandparents and my grandparents are both correct in this context. *Tes* is the possessive plural adjective meaning your. *Ma* is correct because *leçon* is a singular feminine noun.

6.6 Demonstrative Adjectives ("This," "These")

As the name indicates, these adjectives indicate which of several objects or people are being singled out.

Masculine singular: *Ce livre est bon.*

Feminine singular: *Cette jupe me plaît.*

Masculine and **feminine plural:** *Ces hommes, ces femmes sont jeunes.*

Note: Before a **masculine singular** noun with an initial vowel, use *cet:*

cet arbre; cet homme; cet état; cet article

The **plural** of *cet* is *ces:*

ces arbres; ces articles; etc.

Before a **feminine singular** noun with an initial vowel, use *cette:*

cette industrie; cette école; cette amie

The **plural** of *cette* is *ces:*

ces écoles; ces amies; etc.

Note: You may add *–ci* or *–là* to the noun to indicate if the object is closer or farther away:

Ce village-ci est plus grand que ce village-là. This town (here) is larger than that one (there).

Problem Solving Example:

 Fill in the blanks with the appropriate demonstrative adjective.

1. *As-tu vu _____ chat?*
2. *Oui, mais est-ce que tu as vu _____ chiens?*
3. *Penses-tu que _____ robe est belle?*
4. *Non, pas trop . . . je préfère _____ pantalon.*
5. *On parle de quelqu'un de beau. C'est _____ homme?*
6. *Mme Machin m'a donné des fruits . . . _____ pommes, par exemple.*

 1. *As-tu vu **ce** chat?*
2. *Oui, mais est-ce que tu as vu **ces** chiens?*
3. *Penses-tu que **cette** robe est belle?*
4. *Non, pas trop . . . je préfère **ce** pantalon.*
5. *On parle de quelqu'un de beau. C'est **cet** homme?*
6. *Mme Machin m'a donné des fruits . . . **ces** pommes, par exemple.*

6.7 Interrogative Adjectives

To ask "which" or "which one" of a group of things, use *quel, quelle,* or *quels* and *quelles.*

Quel jour sommes-nous? What day is it?

Quelle plage préfères-tu? Which beach do you prefer?

Quels amis t'ont téléphoné? Which friends phoned you?

Quelles chansons vont-ils présenter? Which songs will they perform?

Note: *Quel* may also be an exclamation:

Quelle belle femme! What a beautiful woman!

Quels problèmes! What problems!

Problem Solving Example:

Fill in the blanks with the appropriate interrogative adjective.

1. _____ *film avez-vous aimé le plus?*
2. *Alors, tu peux travailler* _____ *jours?*
3. _____ *actrice a joué le rôle principal?*
4. _____ *revues de cinéma lisent-ils?*
5. *De* _____ *livre est-ce que le prof parle?*

1. ***Quel*** *film avez-vous aimé le plus?*
2. *Alors, tu peux travailler* ***quels*** *jours?*
3. ***Quelle*** *actrice a joué le rôle principal?*
4. ***Quelles*** *revues de cinéma lisent-ils?*
5. *De* ***quel*** *livre est-ce que le prof parle?*

6.8 Adjectives of Number

Cardinal numbers are invariable, except for *un*, *vingt*, and *cent*, which under certain conditions agree with the noun they modify:

Il a écrit quatre-vingts articles. He wrote 80 articles. **But:**

Il a écrit quatre-vingt-trois articles. He wrote 83 articles.

Il y a seulement une femme dans la chambre. There is only one woman in the room. **But:**

Il y a deux femmes dans la chambre. There are two women in the room.

Son manteau coûte deux cents dollars. Her coat costs $200. **But:**

Cela coûte deux cent cinq dollars. This costs $205 dollars.

Remember that if the number is more than 200, there is no agreement. "S" is put onto *cent* only when there is not another number following it:

trois cents / *trois cent trois*

300   303

6.9 *Demi(e)*: Half

When *demi* is used in expressions of time, it should agree with the gender of the noun it reflects.

*Le train arrivera à **une heure et demie**.* The train will arrive at 1:30. *"Demie"* agrees with *"heure,"* which is feminine.

*Nous déjeunons à **midi et demi**.* We have lunch at 12:30. *"Demi"* agrees with *"midi,"* which is masculine.

However, when *demi* **precedes** the noun it reflects, it is always **masculine.**

J'ai travaillé une demi-journée. I worked a half-day.

6.10 Indefinite Adjectives

As the name indicates, they describe a generalized and non-specific noun:

Indefinite Adjectives

Masculine	Feminine	Definition, Example
Singular: *tout*	*toute*	All of **one** class of things: *tout le monde; toute la famille; tout le livre* (the entire, or whole, book). The verb is **singular.**

Plural: *tous*	*toutes*	*Tous mes amis; toutes les chansons.* The verb is **plural.**
plusieurs	*plusieurs*	Several: *plusieurs amis/ amies.*
quelque(s)	*quelque(s)*	Some, a few: *quelque temps; quelque part; quelques cartes.*
aucun (sing. only)	*aucune*	Not one, no: *aucun cadeau; aucune femme.*
certain(s)	*certaine(s)*	Certain, some: *certaines personnes; certains jours.*
chaque	*chaque*	Each, every: *chaque jour; chaque fois.*
différent(s)	*différente(s)*	Different: *Il y a de différents livres; de différentes femmes.*
n'importe quel(s)	*n'importe quelle(s)*	Any . . . whatsoever: *Vous trouverez de bons vins dans n'importe quelle région de France.*

Problem Solving Example:

 Choose the correct demonstrative and indicative forms in parentheses:

Q: *(**Quels**, **Quelles**) genres de livres aimez vous lire? Il y a de (**différents**, **différentes**) livres. Tous mes amis (**aime**, **amient**) lire. (**Certains**, **Certaines**) jours Josette aime beaucoup les livres romantiques. Elle a lu (**vingt-deux**, **vingts-deux**) livres dans une année. J'espère la voir dans (**une heure demie**, **une heure et demie**). (**Plusieurs**, **Plusieures**) personnes vont venir aussi.*

*Quels genres de livres aimez-vous lire? Il y a de **différents** livres. Tous mes amis **aiment** lire. **Certains** jours Josette aime beaucoup les livres romantiques. Elle a lu **vingt-deux** livres dans une année. J'espère la voir dans **une heure et demie**. **Plusieurs** personnes vont venir aussi.*

Quels is the plural masculine adjective modifying *genres* and it means "what" or "which" in English. *Différents* modifies *livres*, which is a plural masculine noun. *Aiment* is correct because *tous* is plural and takes a plural verb. *Certains* modifies the masculine plural noun *jours*. *Vingt-deux* is correct because cardinal numbers are invariable. *Une heure et demie* is feminine and *demie* agrees with *heure*, which is a feminine noun used when speaking of half-hours. *Plusieurs* is correct because it is used with both masculine and feminine nouns invariably.

CHAPTER 7

Pronouns

7.1 Subject Pronouns

Pronouns take the place of nouns and have many functions in French. **Personal pronouns** may replace persons or things and act as **subjects, direct,** or **indirect objects.**

Subject pronouns perform the action of the verb.

First Person

Je	I
nous	we (masc. or fem.)

Je fais le travail. I do the work.
Nous l'aimons. We like it.

Second Person

tu	you (masc. or fem., familiar)
vous	you (singular, formal)
vous	you (plural)

Tu danses bien. You dance well.
Vous partez tôt. You're leaving early.

Third Person

il	he, it (masc.)
elle	she, it (fem.)
on	one, everyone, we, you, they (indef.)
ils	they (masc. plural or masc. and fem. plural: *Jean et Marie = ils*)
elles	they (fem. plural)

Elle est malade. She's sick.
Ils comprennent tout. They understand everything.

7.2 Direct Object Pronouns

Direct object pronouns **receive** the action of the verb **directly** without any interference from another person or object.

First Person

me	me (masc. or fem.)
nous	us (masc. or fem.)

*Edgar **me** déteste.* Edgar hates me.
*Mon ami **nous** invite.* My friend's inviting us.

Second Person

te	you (masc. or fem., familiar)
vous	you (masc. or fem., singular or plural)

*Sam **t'**aime.* Sam loves you.
*Irma **vous** regarde.** Irma's looking at you.

Third Person

le	him, it (masc.)
la	her, it (fem.)
les	them (masc. or fem. plural)

*Je cherche **le** chat. Je **le** cherche.** I'm looking for the cat. I'm looking for him.

*Il voit **la** table. Il **la** voit.* He sees the table. He sees it.

*Tu fais **les** exercices. Tu **les** fais.* You're doing the exercises. You're doing them.

*J'écoute la radio. Je **l'**écoute.** I listen to the radio. I listen to it.
*J'attends l'autobus. Je **l'**attends.** I'm waiting for the bus. I'm waiting for it.

* Note: ***Regarder*** (to look at) and ***chercher*** (to look or search for) take a **direct object** in French. Similarly, ***écouter*** (to listen to) and ***attendre*** (to wait for) take **direct objects.**

Problem Solving Example:

Replace each of the following expressions in bold with a direct object pronoun.

1. *J'écoute **le disque de Serge Gainsbourg.***
2. *Tu attends **ta sœur**, j'imagine.*
3. *Martine cherche **son chat.***
4. *Georges fait **ses exercises de français** tous les jours.*
5. *Tu vas inviter **Jean et moi**?*

1. *Je **l'**écoute.*
2. *Tu **l'**attends, j'imagine.*
3. *Martine **le** cherche.*
4. *Georges **les** fait tous les jours.*
5. *Tu vas **nous** inviter?*

7.2.1 Position in Sentence

Object pronouns **precede** the verb. Whereas in English, the word order is **subject–verb–object** (I see you.), in French, it is **subject–object–verb** *(Je te vois.)*.

7.3 Indirect Object Pronouns

Indirect object pronouns include the preposition *à* (to) in their meaning. Only the third person pronouns change for indirect objects; *me, te, nous, vous* appear in the same forms for direct and indirect objects.

First Person

me (to me)   *Gaston m'a parlé.*
         Gaston spoke to me.
nous (to us)   *Marie nous a envoyé de fleurs.*
         Marie sent us flowers. **OR** Marie sent flowers to us.

Second Person

te (to you)   *Il va t'écrire.*
                    He's going to write to you.
vous (to you)   *Elle vous donne un cadeau.*
                    She gives you a gift. **OR** She gives a gift to you.

Third Person

lui (to him, to her)   *Paul lui a parlé.*
                          Paul spoke to her.
leur (to them)   *Elle veut leur téléphoner.*
                          She wants to call them.

Note: *Téléphoner à quelqu'un* takes an indirect object in French.

The third person indirect object *leur* is invariable. Do not confuse it with the possessive adjective *leur mère* (their mother) or *leurs amis* (their friends).

Hint: Just as the word indirect is longer than the word direct, third person indirect object pronouns are longer than direct object pronouns.

7.3.1 Position of Indirect Object Pronouns

As with direct object pronouns, indirect object pronouns **precede** the verb:

*Nous **lui** envoyons une lettre.* We're sending him (or her) a letter.

*Nancy répond à ses cousins. Elle **leur** répond.* Nancy answers her cousins. She answers them.

Note: *"Répondre à"* takes an **indirect object.**

Problem Solving Example:

Replace each of the following italicized expressions with an indirect object pronoun.

1. *Marie donne des bonbons à **Jacques**.*
2. *Je parle souvent **à mes parents**.*
3. *Jean-Jacques écrit **à Jeanne et à moi**.*
4. *Olivier téléphone **à toi et à Guillaume**.*
5. *Dominique envoie des fleurs **à ses copines**.*

6. *Ma cousine va inviter à **nous**.*
7. *Je vais écrire une lettre à Marie pour dire **à Marie que je pense à elle**.*

1. *Marie **lui** donne des bonbons.*
2. *Je **leur** parle souvent.*
3. *Jean-Jacques **nous** écrit.*
4. *Olivier **vous** téléphone.*
5. *Dominique **leur** envoie des fleurs.*
6. Ma cousine **va nous inviter.**
7. *Je vais **lui écrire** une lettre pour lui dire que je pense à elle.*

7.4 With Two Verbs Together

With two verbs together, place the object pronoun **before the infinitive:**

*Il veut faire ce dîner. Il veut **le** faire.* He wants to make dinner. He wants to make it.

*Margot va **lui** écrire.* Margot will write to him.

Problem Solving Example:

Answer the following questions by replacing the bold words with a direct or indirect object pronoun.

1. *Est-ce que Mark a acheté **son livre**?*

   Oui, il _____.

2. *As-tu aimé **ce film**?*

   Non, je _____.

3. *Est-ce que Paul parle souvent **à sa mère**?*

   Oui, il _____.

4. *Avez-vous téléphoné **à vos professeurs**?*

   Oui, je _____.

5. *Est-ce que tu vas manger **cette pomme**?*

   Oui, je _____.

1. *Oui, il **l'**a acheté.*
2. *Non, je ne **l'**ai pas aimé.*
3. *Oui, il **lui** parle souvent.*
4. *Oui, je **leur** ai téléphoné.*
5. *Oui, je vais **la** manger.*

Remember that indirect and direct object pronouns precede the verb that they modify—whether or not the verb is conjugated.

7.5   With Two Object Pronouns Together

When two object pronouns are in the same sentence, they appear in this order before the verb:

> *Me, te, se, nous, vous* are always first.
> *Le, la, les* follow next.
> *Lui, leur* are always last.

*Il donne son livre à moi. Il **me le** donne.*
*Paul envoie vos cadeaux à vous. Paul **vous les** envoie.*
*Bill vend sa voiture à Mireille. Il **la lui** vend.*
*Elle offre ces photos à ses parents. Elle **les leur** offre.*

Problem Solving Example:

Replace each of the following italicized expressions with a direct object pronoun and an indirect object pronoun.

1. *Tu as donné **les biscuits à ta sœur**, n'est-ce pas?*
2. *Patrick raconte **l' histoire à son petit fils**.*
3. *J'envoie **les cadeaux à mes parents** quand je ne vais pas chez eux pour Noël.*
4. *Vous offrez **le poste à la personne de mon âge**.*
5. *Elle vend **l'auto à la nouvelle cliente**.*

1. *Tu les lui as donnés, n'est-ce pas?*
2. *Patrick me la raconte.*
3. *Je les leur envoie quand je ne vais pas chez eux pour Noël.*
4. *Vous le lui offrez.*
5. *Elle la lui vend.*

7.6 Y and *en*; *Penser à*; *Parler de*

Y and *en* replace things, places, ideas, or expressions, but do not replace people.

Y replaces prepositional phrases of location.

Y can also replace expressions in which the object of the preposition *à* is a thing.

Y can never refer to a person.

Il va à l'aéroport. Il y va. He's going to the airport. He's going there. (Prepositional phrase of location)

Les fleurs sont sur la table. Elles y sont. The flowers are on the table. They're on it. (Prepositional phrase of location)

Nous avons mis son argent dans le tiroir. Nous y avons mis son argent. We put his money in the drawer. We put his money there. (Prepositional phrase of location)

Elle a répondu à ta question. Elle y a répondu. She answered your question. She answered it. (Object of the preposition *à* is a thing.)

Les bons citoyens obéissent aux lois. Ils y obéissent. Good citizens obey the laws. They obey them. (Object of preposition *à* is a thing.)

Note for *penser*:

Penser à + a thing = to think about something:

Il pense à son voyage. Il y pense. He thinks about his trip. He's thinking about it.

Note:

Penser à + a person = disjunctive pronoun (see 7.8 for further information about disjunctive pronouns):

*Je pense à mon père. Je pense à **lui.*** I think about my father. I'm thinking about him.

En replaces expressions with *de*. ***En*** also replaces nouns that are preceded by a number or description of quantity:

*Ma sœur revient **de Paris**. Elle **en** revient.* My sister's returning from Paris. She's returning from there.

*A-t-il parlé **de ses aventures?** Oui, il **en** a parlé.* Did he speak about his adventures? Yes, he spoke about them.

*Il parle souvent **de ses problèmes**. Il **en** parle souvent.* He often talks about his problems. He often talks about them.

When ***en*** replaces nouns preceded by numbers or quantities, the noun is replaced but the number or quantity remains in the sentence:

*Il a pris cinq verres. Il **en** a pris cinq.* He had five drinks. He had five of them.

*As-tu beaucoup **de temps libre?** Non, je **n'en ai pas** beaucoup.* Do you have a lot of free time? I don't have a lot.

*Jean-François a onze cousins. Il **en** a onze.*

Jean-François has eleven cousins. He has eleven of them.

Note: The verb *parler* + *de* + an idea, place, or thing = *en:*

*Sam parle de son travail. Il **en** parle.* Sam talks about his work. He talks about it.

But: *parler de* + a person = a disjunctive pronoun:

*Sam **parle de ses parents**. Il parle **d'eux**.* Sam is talking about his parents. He's talking about them.

Note: *parler à* + a person = indirect object pronoun:

*Sam **parle à sa petite amie**. Il **lui** parle.* Sam is talking to his girlfriend. He's talking **to** her.

Resumé:

1. Use *y* to replace expressions with *à* and other prepositions (besides *de*).

2. Use *en* to replace expressions with *de*.

3. The verbs *penser* and *parler* make a distinction between pronouns that replace things or people.

   a. *Penser à* + a thing = *y*

   b. *Penser à* + a person = disjunctive pronoun (*à moi, à lui*, etc.)

   c. *Penser de:* This form is used only **in a question** seeking an **opinion**. *Que penses-tu de mon chapeau? Qu'en penses-tu?* Answer: *Je pense qu'il est chic.*

   d. *Penser de* + a person = disjunctive pronoun. *Que penses-tu de Jean? Que penses-tu de lui?* Answer: *Je pense qu'il est gentil.*

Word order with *y* and *en*: These two pronouns come after direct and indirect object pronouns; *y* precedes *en*.

Je mets les stylos dans la boîte. Je les y mets. I put them there.

Tu as donné de l'argent à Pierre. Tu lui en as donné. You gave him some.

Note: There is never any agreement with *en*.

Nous leur avons envoyé des fleurs. Nous leur en avons envoyé. We've sent them some (flowers).

Hint: Remember, the expression *"Il y en a,"* which answers the question *"Y a-t-il (des roses sur la table)?"* — *Oui, il y en a.*

Problem Solving Examples:

Choose the correct pronoun form (either *y* or *en*) by filling in the blank.

Sophie est une de mes cousines. Je pense bien souvent à elle et aux belles vacances que nous avons passées ensemble chez elle. Je me suis promise d'_____ retourner bientôt.

Sophie est une de mes cousines. Je pense bien souvent à elle et aux belles vacances que nous avons passées ensemble chez elle. Je me suis promise d'y retourner bientôt.

The pronouns *y* and *en* can replace places, things, or ideas, but they can never replace people. Because we know that the narrator of this paragraph is talking about time spent at Sophie's house, *chez elle*, we can assume that the narrator has promised to return *chez elle*. This is a prepositional phrase of location. *Y* is the correct answer because it represents phrases of location.

Answer the following questions while replacing the italicized expressions with either the pronoun "*y*" or "*en*."

1. *Allez-vous à la banque aujourd'hui?*
   Oui, _____ .
2. *Est-ce que tu gardes des souvenirs de tes vacances au lac Léman?*
   Oui, _____ .
3. *On dîne bien chez vous, n'est-ce pas?*
   Oui, _____ .
4. *Elle a fait deux voyages en France. Comment? Combien de voyages est-ce qu'elle a fait en France?*
   Elle _____ .
5. *Avez-vous peur de prendre l'avion?*
   Oui, _____ .

1. *Oui, j'y vais aujourd'hui.*
2. *Oui, j'en garde des souvenirs.*
3. *Oui, on y dîne bien.*
4. *Elle en a fait deux.*
5. *Oui, j'en ai peur.*

7.7 Interrogative Sentences with Pronouns

As with declarative sentences, pronouns **precede the verb** in **interrogative** sentences:

Avons-nous assez d'argent? En avons-nous assez?* Do we have enough money?

Est-ce que tu connais Marcie? Est-ce que tu la connais? Do you know her?

Ont-ils pris mon stylo? L'ont-ils pris? Did they take it?

Pierre est-il à New York maintenant? Y est-il? Is he there?

*Note: The **adverb** *"assez"* is repeated.

7.8 Disjunctive Pronouns

Disjunctive pronouns are **not joined** to the verb, as are those discussed so far. Their forms are: *moi, toi, lui, elle, nous, vous, eux, elles.* Their principal uses are:

a. After a preposition: *Je vais chez toi. Le livre est devant lui.*

b. After *c'est: Qui parle? C'est elle. C'est lui.*

c. With a double subject: *Simon et moi, nous allons à Paris.*

d. With *parler de* + **a person.** *Je parle de mes amis. Je parle d'eux.*

e. With *penser à* + **a person** and *penser de* + **a person.**

f. To emphasize a strong statement: *Moi, j'ai dit cela?* I said that?

g. To compare and contrast two elements: *Paul, lui, est riche mais Marie, elle, est pauvre.*

Problem Solving Example:

Rewrite the following sentences, replacing the noun in bold with a disjunctive pronoun.

1. *Il n'aime que Marie.*
2. *Vous parlez toujours de Jacques et de Ludovic?*
3. *Je n'ai vu ni David ni les Duro.*
4. *Qui est là? C'est le policier.*
5. *Nous allons dîner chez Marie ce soir.*

1. *Il n'aime qu'elle.*
2. *Vous parlez toujours d'eux?*
3. *Je n'ai vu ni lui ni eux.*
4. *Qui est là? C'est lui.*
5. *Nous allons dîner chez elle ce soir.*

7.9 Relative Pronouns

Relative pronouns link or relate two ideas or two clauses. They must have an **antecedent** (a noun or pronoun that comes before the pronoun and to which it refers).

7.9.1 Simple Relative Pronouns

Simple relative pronoun forms: *qui* (subject), *que* (object), and *où* (for places and time).

Nous regardons l'homme qui danse si bien. We're watching the man who dances so well. *Qui* links the two ideas and is the **subject** of the verb *danse.* Antecedent: *l'homme.*

Le livre que tu cherchais a disparu. The book for which you were looking has disappeared. *Que* is the **object** of the verb *chercher.* Antecedent: *le livre.*

Voilà le café où Bill travaille. There's the café where Bill works. *Où* designates **"the place where."** Antecedent: *le café.*

Minuit est l'heure où nous nous couchons. Midnight is the time (when) we go to bed. Antecedent: *l'heure.*

Hint: To differentiate **subject** from **object,** remember that *qui* always **precedes the verb directly;** *que* always has **another subject before the verb.**

7.9.2 Ce Qui, Ce Que

Ce qui, ce que are used in sentences where there is **no antecedent.** *Ce* = "the thing that" or "what":

Tu ne sais pas ce qui est bon. You don't know what's good.

Je comprends ce que Sam dit. I understand what Sam is saying.

7.9.3 *Lequel, Laquelle, Lesquels, Lesquelles*

Unlike the simple relative pronouns, *lequel* is a relative pronoun used only after a preposition. It always replaces a thing. *Lequel* must agree in gender and number with its antecedent (*lequel, laquelle, lesquels, lesquelles*).

> *C'est le stylo avec lequel le Président a signé la loi.* That's the pen with which the President signed the law.

> *Où est la maison dans laquelle tu habitais?* Where's the house in which you used to live?

> *Voici les voitures sans lesquels nous ne pouvons pas partir.* Here are the cars without which we cannot leave.

When it is preceded by the preposition *à* or *de*, contractions are made: *auquel, auxquels, auxquelles, duquel, desquels, desquelles.*

> *Le grand banquet auquel elle a assisté était marveileux.* The big banquet she attended was astonishing.

> *Je n'ai rien à dire au sujet duquel vous parlez.* I don't have anything to say about the subject of which you are speaking.

There are two cases in which *lequel* can be used to replace people:

After the adverb *parmi:*

> *Voilà des étudiants parmi lesquels se trouve ta cousine.* There are some students, among whom is your cousin.

When there is a need to emphasize or clarify the gender or number of the antecedent:

> *Connaissez-vous les enfants pour lesquelles il a écrit ses poèmes?* Do you know the children for whom he wrote his poems?

Because *enfants* is invariable, we only know the gender of the children from the feminine for *lesquelles*.

7.9.4 *Dont*

Dont is the relative pronoun used to replace *de*. *Dont* is used to replace people in phrases with *de*. It is also regularly used instead of *duquel, de laquelle*, etc. to replace things:

La personne dont vous parlez n'est pas en ville. The person of whom you're speaking is not in town.

J'ai dîné au restaurant dont mes parents parlent de temps en temps. I dined at the restaurant of which my parents speak from time to time.

Remember that in French you cannot end a sentence with a preposition. Use *dont* to avoid ending a sentence with *de*:

C'est le livre dont j'ai besoin.

It's the book that I need.

*To replace a person after a preposition other than *de* use *qui*.

Voilà la fille avec qui j'ai parlé.

There's the girl with whom I spoke.

Dont also acts as a relative pronoun meaning "whose":

Yves, dont le frère est Paul, comprend la situation. Yves, whose brother is Paul, understands the situation.

C'est l'étudiant dont l'examen n'était pas lisible. It's the student whose exam wasn't legible.

Ce dont is used when there is **no antecedent** (the thing about which, the thing of which) and when *de* is being replaced in the sentence:

Je ne comprends pas ce dont vous avez besoin. [*avoir besoin + de*]. I don't understand what you need.

Ce dont ils parlent me fait peur. [*parler + de*]. What they are talking about frightens me.

Problem Solving Example:

Fill in the blanks with the correct relative pronouns.

1. *Voici les gens _____ j'ai rencontrés à Dijon.*
2. *Nous avons pris un bus _____ était plein de touristes.*
3. *C'est la gare _____ nous sommes arrivés.*

4. *Voilá le parc dans _____ nous nous sommes promenés.*
5. *Voici la personne _____ la sœur travaille à Besançon.*
6. *Je ne veux pas te raconter tout _____ nous avons fait pendant nos vacances.*
7. *_____ m'a tellement impressionné à Cannes, c'est la beauté de la mer!*
8. *Enfin, voici quelques plages sur _____ nous avons fait la connaissance de quelques enfants.*
9. *Voici l'homme italien _____ j'ai fait la connaissance sur la plage naturiste.*
10. *Il y a des membres de notre groupe à _____ j'écris toujours.*

1. *Voici les gens **que** j'ai recontrés a Dijon.*
2. *Nous avons pris un bus **qui** était plein de touristes.*
3. *C'est la gare **où** nous sommes arrivés.*
4. *Voilà le parc dans **lequel** nous nous sommes promenés.*
5. *Voici la personne **dont** la soeur travaille à Besançon.*
6. *Je ne veux pas te raconter tout **ce que** nous avons fait pendant nos vacances.*
7. ***Ce que** m'a tellement impressionné à Cannes, c'est la beauté de la mer!*
8. *Enfin, voici quelques plages sur **lesquelles** nous avons fait la connaissance de quelques enfants.*
9. *Voici l'homme italien **dont** j'ai fait la connaissance sur **la plage** naturiste.*
10. *Il y a des membres de notre groupe à **qui** j'écris toujours.*

7.10 Possessive Pronouns

Possessive pronouns take the place of nouns and agree with them in number and gender.

7.10.1 Forms of Possessive Pronouns

Remember that the pronoun agrees with the object possessed, **not with the gender of the possessor.**

First Person	**Second Person**	**Third Person**
le mien – mine, m. sing.	*le tien* – yours, m. sing.	*le sien* – his, hers, m. sing.
les miens –mine, m. pl.	*les tiens* – yours, m. pl.	*les siens* – his, hers
le nôtre – ours, m. sing.	*le vôtre* – yours, m. sing.	*le leur* – theirs, m. sing.
la mienne– mine, f. sing.	*la tienne* – yours, f. sing.	*la sienne* – his, hers, f. sing.
les miennes – mine, f. pl.	*les tiennes* – yours, f. pl.	*les siennes* – his, hers, f. pl.
les nôtres – ours, m. or f. pl.	*les vôtres* – yours, pl.	*les leurs* – theirs, m. or f. pl.
la nôtre – ours, f. sing.	*la vôtre* – yours, f. sing.	*la leur* – theirs, f. sing

Où sont tes amis? **Les miens** *sont ici.* Where are your friends? Mine are here.

Ta robe est jolie. **La sienne** *est laide.* Your dress is pretty. Hers is ugly.

Nos oncles sont là. **Les leurs** *sont partis.* Our uncles are here. Theirs left.

Problem Solving Example:

Using the cues of the objects and their owners, complete the sentences to show ownership by using a possessive pronoun.

1. *la veste à vous; J'ai oublié ma veste. Donnez-moi _____.*
2. *le livre à Jacques; Je n'ai plus de livre. Passe-moi _____.*
3. *les billets aux étudiants; Est-ce que ce sont mes billets ou _____?*
4. *la tasse de café à moi; Marishka ne trouve plus sa tasse de café; est-ce que c'est _____?*
5. *la voiture à papa; Ma voiture est en panne; puis-je utiliser _____?*
6. *les chambres à nous; Mais il y a du monde chez nous*

pendant ces vacances! Y-a-t-il assez de chambres pour héberger nos invités? Mes cousins peuvent dormir dans _____.

7. *les CD aux Coignet; J'ai perdu mon CD de Brel. Par hasard, est-ce que c'est parmi* _____.

8. *l'argent de poche à mon frère; Lucie n'a pas assez d'argent pour acheter tous ces bonbons…elle se souvient de* _____.

9. *la copine à David; Je ne savais pas que Thérèse est la copine de David. C'est vrai? Elle est* _____.

10. *le chien à Arnaud et à Jérémy; C'est à qui, ce sacré chien qui aboie. Demande à Arnaud et à Jérémy. C'est* _____?

1. *J'ai oublié ma veste. Donnez-moi* **la vôtre.**
2. *Je n'ai plus de livre. Passe-moi* **le sien.**
3. *Est-ce que ce sont mes billets ou* **les leurs?**
4. *Marishka ne trouve plus sa tasse de café; est-ce que c'est* **la mienne?**
5. *Ma voiture est en panne; puis-je utiliser* **la sienne?**
6. *Mais il y a du monde chez nous pendant ces vacances! Y-a-t-il assez de chambres pour héberger nos invités? Mes cousins peuvent dormir dans* **les nôtres.**
7. *J'ai perdu mon CD de Brel. Par hasard, est-ce que c'est parmi* **les leurs?**
8. *Lucie n'a pas assez d'argent pour acheter tous ces bonbons . . . elle se souvient* **du sien.**
9. *Je ne savais pas que Thérèse est la copine de David. C'est vrai? Elle est* **la sienne.**
10. *C'est à qui, ce sacré chien qui aboie? Demande à Arnaud et à Jérémy. C'est* **le leur?**

Quiz: Adjectives and Pronouns

1. Voilà la personne ———— va jouer du piano.

    (A) que   (C) ce que

    (B) qui   (D) ce qui

2. C'est sa mère avec _____ vous venez de parler.

    (A) lequel   (C) qui

    (B) laquelle   (D) que

3. Son piano a un beau son mais je préfère le mien parce que j'_____ suis habituée.

    (A) y   (C) a

    (B) en   (D) ai

4. J'ai besoin de téléphoner à mes parents. Je veux _____ téléphoner.

    (A) nous   (C) leur

    (B) les   (D) leurs

5. Cette histoire est bonne, mais l'autre est **plus intéressante**.

    (A) mieux   (C) meilleure

    (B) le meilleur   (D) meilleur

6. Tes cousins vont-ils venir à la fête avec **tes** amis?

    (A) vos   (C) leurs

    (B) leur   (D) ses

7. Le problème **dont** il parle est très sérieux.

    (A) de qui   (C) de quoi

    (B) duquel   (D) de laquelle

Directions: Fill in the blanks of the following conversation using the appropriate word.

---

8. J'ai perdu _____ stylo…

    (A) mon   (C) le mien

    (B) ma   (D) la mienne

9. . . . voulez-vous bien me prêter _____ ?

    (A) le tien   (C) le mien

    (B) le vôtre   (D) la mienne

10. Oui, certainement, servez-vous _____ .

    (A) à la mienne   (C) du mien

    (B) de la mienne (D) au mien

ANSWER KEY

1.	(B)	6.	(C)
2.	(C)	7.	(B)
3.	(A)	8.	(A)
4.	(C)	9.	(B)
5.	(C)	10.	(C)

CHAPTER 8

Verbs

8.1 *L'indicatif*

Verbs are the heart of the sentence and **express an action or a state of being, mental or physical.** There are several **moods** of verbs (means of communication) and each mood contains **tenses** (time of the action). *L'indicatif, l'impératif, le conditionnel,* and *le subjonctif* are the principal moods we will discuss.

L'indicatif (the indicative) indicates or relates information in either declarative or interrogative sentences. It has three main conjugations: *–er, –ir,* or *–re* verbs. The *infinitif* (the "to" form) is made up of **a stem + an ending.**

8.1.1 Regular *–er* Verbs

Regular *–er* verbs: *chanter, danser, manger, donner, parler,* etc.

Note: The great majority of French verbs are of this conjugation.

Present tense of *chanter* (to sing). *Chant* = stem (or radical) + *er* = ending.

Present participle = *chantant* (singing)

je chante	*nous chantons*
(I sing, I am singing, I do sing)	
tu chantes	*vous chantez*
il (elle, on) chante	*ils (elles) chantent*

8.1.2 *–ir* Verbs

There are two classes of *–ir* verbs, those that add *-iss-* to the plural forms *(maigrir, finir, choisir, réussir, fleurir, brunir)* and those that do not *(dormir, sortir, partir)*. The **present participles** of *finir = finissant* (finishing) and *dormir = dormant* (sleeping) also reflect these differences.

Finir:

je finis	*nous finissons*
tu finis	*vous finissez*
il finit	*ils finissent (elles)*
to il (elle, on)	

Dormir:

je dors	*nous dormons*
tu dors	*vous dormez*
il (elle) dort	*ils (elles) dorment*
to il (elle, on)	

8.1.3 Regular *–re* Verbs

Regular verbs ending in *–re (vendre, rendre, attendre, descendre):*

Attendre (to wait for)   **present participle: *attendant***

j'attends	*nous attendons*
tu attends	*vous attendez*
il (elle) attend	*ils (elles) attendent*

8.1.4 Verbs Ending in *–oir*

Verbs ending in *–oir (voir, recevoir, pouvoir, vouloir, devoir,* etc.) are irregular but commonly follow a pattern: 1st, 2nd, 3rd persons singular and 3rd person plural are **similar:**

Voir (to see)   **present participle: *voyant***

je vois	*nous voyons*
tu vois	*vous voyez*
il (elle) voit	*ils (elles) voient*

Vouloir (to want, to wish)   **present participle:** *voulant*

je veux	*nous voulons*
tu veux	*vous voulez*
il (elle) veut	*ils (elles) veulent*

Recevoir (to receive)   **present participle:** *recevant*

je reçois	*nous recevons*
tu reçois	*vous recevez*
il (elle) reçoit	*ils (elles) reçoivent*

Note: No cedilla is used under the "c" when it is before "e."

8.1.5   Spelling Changes in *–er* Verbs

Some otherwise regular *–er* verbs have **spelling changes** in the *nous* and *vous* forms:

appeler:	*j'appelle*	*nous appelons*	*vous appelez*
jeter:	*je jette*	*nous jetons*	*vous jetez*
acheter:	*j'achète*	*nous achetons*	*vous achetez*
espérer:	*j'espère*	*nous espérons*	*vous espérez*
préférer:	*je préfère*	*nous préférons*	*vous préférez*
manger:	*je mange*	*nous mangeons**	*vous mangez*

*Manger (ranger, changer) takes an extra *"e"* in the *nous* form in order to maintain consistency with pronunciation.

Problem Solving Example:

Give the correct present tense conjugations of the verbs given in parentheses

1. (*aimer*) *Oh! il m'* _____.
2. (*chanter*) *Quand je suis malade, je ne* _____ *pas très bien.*
3. (*manger*) *Nous* _____ *beaucoup pendant les fêtes.*
4. (*choisir*) *Elle* _____ *de ne rien faire pendant les vacances.*
5. (*rendre*) *Vous* _____ *visite à votre famille ce week-end, n'est-ce pas?*

6. *(descendre) Tu* _____ *à la cave chercher du vin assez souvent.*
7. *(jeter) Nous* _____ *plein de choses dans la poubelle.*
8. *(appeler) Vous* _____ *Marie et Jeanne tout le temps!*
9. *(devoir) Je* _____ *manger plus tôt ce soir.*
10. *(pouvoir) Tu ne* _____ *pas rentrer trop tard ce soir.*

1. *Oh! Il m'aime.*
2. *Quand je suis malade, je ne* **chante** *pas très bien.*
3. *Nous* **mangeons** *beaucoup pendant les fêtes.*
4. *Elle* **choisit** *de ne rien faire pendant les vacances.*
5. *Vous* **rendez** *visite à votre famille ce week-end, n'est-ce pas?*
6. *Tu* **descends** *à la cave chercher du vin assez souvent.*
7. *Nous* **jetons** *plein de choses dans la poubelle.*
8. *Vous* **appelez** *Marie et Jeanne tout le temps!*
9. *Je* **dois** *manger plus tôt ce soir.*
10. *Tu ne* **peux** *pas rentrer trop tard ce soir.*

8.1.6 Common Irregular Verbs

Common irregular verbs (with present participle)

Être (étant)

je suis	nous sommes
tu es	vous êtes
il (elle) est	ils (elles) sont

Avoir (ayant)

j'ai	nous avons
tu as	vous avez
il (elle) a	ils (elles) ont

Faire (faisant)

je fais	nous faisons
tu fais	vous faites
il (elle) fait	ils (elles) font

Aller (allant)

je vais	nous allons
tu vas	vous allez
il (elle) va	ils (elles) vont

Note: *ils* **ont** *(avoir); ils* **sont** *(être); ils* **font** *(faire); ils* **vont** *(aller)*

Venir (venant)

je viens	nous venons
tu viens	vous venez
il (elle) vient	ils (elles) viennent

Pouvoir (pouvant)

je peux	nous pouvons
tu peux	vous pouvez
il (elle) peut	ils (elles) peuvent

Dire (disant)

je dis	nous disons
tu dis	vous dites
il (elle) dit	ils (elles) disent

Envoyer (envoyant)

j'envoie	nous envoyons
tu envoies	vous envoyez
il (elle) envoie	ils (elles) envoient

Prendre (prenant)

je prends	nous prenons
tu prends	vous prenez
il (elle) prend	ils (elles) prennent

Écrire (écrivant)

j'écris	nous écrivons
tu écris	vous écrivez
il (elle) écrit	ils (elles) écrivent

Craindre (craignant)

je crains	nous craignons
tu crains	vous craignez
il (elle) craint	ils (elles) craignent

Savoir (sachant)

je sais	nous savons
tu sais	vous savez
il (elle) sait	ils (elles) savent

Boire (buvant)

je bois	nous buvons
tu bois	vous buvez
il (elle) boit	ils (elles) boivent

Lire (lisant)

je lis	nous lisons
tu lis	vous lisez
il (elle) lit	ils (elles) lisent

Problem Solving Example:

Give the correct present tense conjugations of the verbs in parentheses.

1. *(être) Nous* _____ *contents de vous voir.*
2. *(avoir) J'* _____ *cinq francs dans ma poche.*
3. *(faire) Il* _____ *du soleil aujourd'hui.*
4. *(aller) Elle* _____ *à l'université.*
5. *(venir) Tu* _____ *avec nous?*
6. *(lire) Je* _____ *tous les romans d'Alain Robbe-Grillet.*
7. *(écrire) Vous* _____ *comme un poulet!*
8. *(prendre) Daniel* _____ *le métro pour voir Maryse.*
9. *(envoyer) Maman m'* _____ *des cadeaux pour Noël.*
10. *(boire) Vous* _____ *trop de coca pendant les repas.*

1. *Nous **sommes** contents de vous voir.*
2. *J'**ai** cinq francs dans ma poche.*
3. *Il **fait** du soleil aujourd'hui.*

4. *Elle **va** à l'université.*
5. *Tu **viens** avec nous?*
6. *Je **lis** tous les romans d'Alain Robbe-Grillet.*
7. *Vous **écrivez** comme un poulet!*
8. *Daniel **prend** le métro pour voir Maryse.*
9. *Maman m'**envoie** des cadeaux pour Noël.*
10. *Vous **buvez** trop de coca pendant les repas.*

8.2 L'impératif

L'impératif, another **mood**, expresses **commands** or **orders**. The *impératif* is formed by using a verb in the present tense of the *tu, nous,* and *vous* forms.

For the informal commands, use the *tu* form.

For the formal commands, use the *vous* form.

For collective commands, use the *nous* form.

8.2.1 Affirmative Commands

To use an **affirmative command**, simply use the present tense verb forms without their pronoun subjects. Note, however, that the "s" of the *tu* form of -*er* verbs is dropped in the *tu* form of the imperative of -*er* verbs.

Réponds, Jim!	Answer, Jim!
Choisis une pomme!	Take an apple!
Rends mon argent!	Give back my money!
Marie, regarde la lune!	Marie, look at the moon!
Donne le stylo à ton papa!	Give your dad the pen!
Va avec Sam!	Go with Sam!
Marchons vite!	Let's walk fast!
Écrivons la lettre!	Let's write the letter!
Fermez la porte!	Close the door!
Finissez le vin!	Finish the wine!
Prenez votre manteau!	Take your coat!

8.2.2 Negative Commands

To form **negative commands** use the same verb forms, but place *ne* in front of the verb and *pas* after it:

Ne réponds pas!	Don't answer!
Ne rends pas mon argent!	Don't give back my money!
Ne fermez pas la porte!	Don't close the door!
Ne prenez pas votre manteau!	Don't take your coat!

8.2.3 Irregular Imperatives

There are only **three irregular imperative forms:**

Avoir: aie, ayons, ayez

Être: sois, soyons, soyez

Savoir: sache, sachons, sachez

N'aie pas peur! Don't be afraid!

Soyez calme! Be calm!

Sachons la vérité! Let's learn the truth!

8.2.4 Imperative + Pronoun

Imperative + pronoun: With **affirmative** commands, use *le, la, les, nous* for **direct objects** and *moi, nous, lui, leur* for **indirect objects.** Place pronouns **after the verb:**

Regarde-le! Look at it!

Mange-les! Eat them!

Fais-le! Do it!

Écrivez-moi! Write to me!

Parlons-lui! Let's speak to him (her)!

8.2.5 With Negative Commands

With negative commands, place the pronoun **before the verb:**

Ne le regarde pas! Don't look at it!

Ne les mange pas! Don't eat them!

Ne le fais pas! Don't do it!

Ne m'écrivez pas! Don't write to me!

Ne lui parlons pas! Don't talk to him.

8.2.6 With Two Pronouns

With two pronouns, place **people** at the end of the sentence for emphasis in **affirmative commands**. Use regular pronoun order in **negative commands**:

Donne-le-moi! Give it to me! **But:** *Ne me le donne pas!*

Envoyez-les-nous! Send them to us! **But:** *Ne nous les envoyez pas!*

Ecrivez-la-leur! Write it to them! **But:** *Ne la leur écrivez pas!*

8.2.7 Y and *en*

Y and *en* follow personal pronouns in both affirmative and negative commands.

Mettez-les-y!	Put them there!
Ne les y mettez pas!	Don't put them there!
Ne lui en parlez pas!	Don't speak to him about it!
Donnes-m'en!	Give me some!
Ne m'en donne pas!	Don't give me any!

Note: When using *y* and *en* in affirmative commands in the *tu* form, the "s" of the *tu* form of -*er* verbs is retained.

	Vas-y!	Go to it!
But:	*N'y va pas!*	Don't go to it!
	Manges-en!	Eat some of it!
But:	*N'en mange pas!*	Don't eat any of it!

Problem Solving Example:

Rewrite the following imperative statements in the negative.

1. *Oubliez le vin pour notre dîner!*
2. *Mangeons vite!*
3. *Téléphonez-nous!*
4. *Dîtes-le-nous!*
5. *Partages-en avec ton frère!*
6. *Fais-le!*
7. *Donne-le-moi.*

1. *N'oubliez pas le vin pour notre dîner!*
2. *Ne mangeons pas vite!*
3. *Ne nous téléphonez pas!*
4. *Ne nous le dîtes pas!*
5. *N'en partage pas avec ton frère!*
6. *Ne le fais pas!*
7. *Ne me le donne pas!*

8.3 *Le Passé Composé*

Le passé composé is a past tense of a verb in the indicative mood. It is used to express a completed action in the past. The name of this tense (compound past) illustrates the fact that it is made up of **more than one part.** (A "simple" verb has only one component.) There are **two parts** to the *passé composé*: an **auxiliary verb** *(avoir* or *être)* and a **past participle,** which is a verb form that **can never stand alone as a verb.** The auxiliary verb is conjugated, but the past participle is invariable.

8.3.1 Formation of the *Passé Composé*

–er **verbs:** To form the past participle, drop the *–er* of the infinitive and add "é."

donner: to give

j'ai donné (I gave, I did give, I have given)   *nous avons donné* (we gave) *tu as donné* (you gave)   *vous avez donné* (you gave)

il (elle) a donné (he/she gave)   *ils (elles) ont donné* (they gave)

Note: *Avoir* is conjugated; the participle is invariable.

–ir verbs: To form the past participle, drop the "r" of the infinitive.

choisir: to choose

j'ai choisi	*nous avons choisi*
tu as choisi	*vous avez choisi*
il (elle) a choisi	*ils (elles) ont choisi*

–re verbs: To form the past participle, drop the *–re* and add "u" to the stem.

vendre: to sell

j'ai vendu	*nous avons vendu*
tu as vendu	*vous avez vendu*
il (elle) a vendu	*ils (elles) ont vendu*

8.3.2 Past Participles of Irregular Verbs

The above patterns apply to all **regular** verbs; for **irregular** verbs, participles must be learned separately. Here is a list of some of the irregular past participles:

avoir: j'ai eu	*être: j'ai été*	*écrire: j'ai écrit*
courir: j'ai couru	*boire: j'ai bu*	*croire: j'ai cru*
dire: j'ai dit	*prendre: j'ai pris*	*ouvrir: j'ai ouvert*
tenir: j'ai tenu	*faire: j'ai fait*	*lire: j'ai lu*
voir: j'ai vu	*savoir: j'ai su*	*vouloir: j'ai voulu*
pouvoir: j'ai pu	*mettre: j'ai mis*	*vivre: j'ai vécu*
recevoir: j'ai reçu	*plaire: j'ai plu*	

Problem Solving Example:

Rewrite the following sentences in the *passé composé*.

1. *Jacqueline donne des cours particuliers aux hommes d'affaires.*
2. *Je mange des gâteaux.*
3. *Nous buvons de l'eau avec nos repas.*
4. *Vous suivez des cours de français.*
5. *Elle lit Bonjour tristesse de Françoise Sagan.*
6. *Je fais une tarte aux pommes.*
7. *Les élèves disent bonjour à leurs profs.*
8. *Maxime écrit des lettres à sa grand-mère.*
9. *Maman me demande d'ouvrir les bouteilles.*
10. *Tu mets la table pour ta mère, n'est-ce pas?*

1. *Jacqueline **a donné** des cours particuliers aux hommes d'affaires.*
2. *J'**ai mangé** des gâteaux.*
3. *Nous **avons bu** de l'eau avec nos repas.*
4. *Vous **avez suivi** des cours de français.*
5. *Elle **a lu** Bonjour tristesse de Françoise Sagan.*
6. *J'**ai fait** une tarte aux pommes.*
7. *Les élèves **ont dit** bonjour à leurs profs.*
8. *Maxime **a écrit** des lettres à sa grand-mère.*
9. *Maman m'**a demandé** d'ouvrir les bouteilles.*
10. *Tu **a mis** la table pour ta mère, n'est-ce pas?*

8.3.3 *L'Accord* (Agreement)

In the *passé composé* with the auxiliary *avoir*, if there is a **direct object** (noun or pronoun) that **precedes** the **verb** the participle must "agree" with the direct object in gender and number (for feminine and plural). Masculine singular objects that precede the verb do not affect the participle.

*Pierre a pris **ces chemises**. (Chemises* is the direct object of *a pris.)*
*Il **les** a **prises**. (Les* is the feminine plural direct object that
precedes the verb; therefore, you add "es" to the participle *pris.)*

*Nous avons vendu **la voiture**. Nous l'avons **vendue**. (Voiture* is feminine singular, *l* replaces *voiture; vendu* must agree; therefore,
you add an "e.")

Note: When the **direct object follows the verb** *(ces chemises, la
voiture)*, the participle is **invariable**.

*As-tu **rencontré Marie**? L'as-tu **rencontrée**?* Did you meet Marie?
Did you meet her?

ATTENTION:

*Nous avons téléphoné à nos amis. Nous **leur** avons **téléphoné**.*
(Agreement is made **only** with the preceding **direct object,** not the
indirect object.)

8.3.4 *Passé Composé* with *Être*

There are about 20 verbs that form the *passé composé* with *être,*
rather than with *avoir.* (cf., "Joy to the world/the Lord **is** come" in Old
English.) These verbs deal with movement:

aller – to go	*parvenir* – to reach or achieve
arriver – to arrive	*rentrer* – to come or go home
descendre – to come down	*rester* – to stay, remain
devenir – to become	*retourner* – to return
entrer – to enter	*revenir* – to come back, return
monter – to go up, climb	*sortir* – to go out
mourir – to die	*tomber* – to fall
naître – to be born	*venir* – to come
partir – to leave, depart	

8.3.5 Agreement with *Être*

The past participle used with *être* must agree in number and gender with the subject.

*Elles **sont nées** à Paris.* They (fem. pl.) were born in Paris.

*Son amie **est morte** hier.* His friend (fem.) died yesterday.

*Nous **sommes arrivés** en retard.* We (fem. pl.) arrived late.

*Mathilde **est tombée** de son lit.* Matilda (fem.) fell from her bed.

Problem Solving Example:

 Rewrite the following sentences in the *passé composé*.

1. *Marie va à la banque vendredi.*
2. *Nous partons en vacances lundi matin.*
3. *Marc, tu deviens médecin quand?*
4. *Elles rentrent chez elles vers minuit.*
5. *J'arrive à l'aéroport Kennedy.*
6. *Vous entrez par la porte à gauche.*
7. *Les bébés Jean et Marie tombent du banc.*
8. *Tu montes dans ta chambre tout de suite!*
9. *Je reste chez moi pendant les fêtes.*
10. *Madeleine vient nous voir.*

1. *Marie **est allée** à la banque vendredi.*
2. *Nous **sommes parti(e)s** en vacances lundi matin.*
3. *Marc, tu **es devenu** médecin quand?*
4. *Elles **sont rentrées** chez elles vers minuit.*
5. *Je **suis arrivé(e)** à l'aéroport Kennedy.*
6. *Vous **êtes entré(es)** par la porte à gauche.*
7. *Les bébés Jean et Marie **sont tombés** du banc.*
8. *Tu **es monté(e)** dans ta chambre tout de suite!*
9. *Je **suis resté(e)** chez moi pendant les fêtes.*
10. *Madeleine **est venue** nous voir.*

8.3.6 Transitive and Intransitive Verbs

Rentrer, sortir, monter, descendre, passer may be used **transitively** (with a direct object) or **intransitively** (with no object.) When they are **transitive verbs,** they take *avoir:*

J'ai rentré la voiture. I brought the car inside.

Marie a monté la rue Diderot. Marie went up Diderot Street.

Bill a descendu les valises. Bill brought the suitcases down.

Yvette m'a passé le pain. Yvette passed me the bread.

Note: Rules of agreement for *avoir* apply to these five verbs when they are **transitive:** The participle agrees with the preceding **direct object.**

Je l'ai rentrée. I brought it (the car) in.

Marie l'a montée. Marie went up it (the street).

Bill les a descendues. Bill brought them (the suitcases) down.

8.3.7   Interrogative in the *Passé Composé*

With *est-ce que:*

Est-ce que Jacques a téléphoné? Est-il passé ce matin? Did Jack call? Did he come by this morning?

With **inversion:**

Jacques a-t-il téléphoné? (Note: In conversation, the structure "*Jacques a téléphoné?*" is more common.)

Où êtes-vous allés, mes amis? Where did you go, my friends?

Tes parents sont-ils partis? Did your folks leave?

8.3.8   Negative

Since all negatives have two parts *(ne . . . pas, ne . . . jamais, ne . . . pas encore,* etc.), place *ne* before the **verb** *(avoir* or *être)* and *pas, plus,* etc. after the verb which is conjugated.

Il n'a pas vu ton chien. He didn't see your dog.

Nous n'avons plus parlé de lui. We didn't speak of him any longer.

Jeanne n'est jamais allée à Nîmes. Jeanne never went to Nîmes.

Pourquoi n'ont-ils pas encore écrit? Why haven't they written yet?

Negative interrogative + object pronoun with *avoir:* (With *être,* the object pronoun is used only in pronominal verb constructions — see below.)

> *A-t-elle mis la robe? Ne l'a-t-elle pas mise?* Did she wear the dress? Didn't she wear it?

> *Les Duval n'ont-ils pas acheté cette maison? Ne l'ont-ils pas achetée?* Didn't the Duvals buy that house? Didn't they buy it?

Problem Solving Example:

In this passage, two choices of verb conjugations are given. Use the correct form.

> *Lucienne travaille dans une chemiserie. Là elle vend naturellement des chemises. Elle faisait même les étalages. Son cousin André (est venu, a venu) et (est acheté, a acheté) des chemises pour son travail de bureau. Il (les a prises, les a pris) car il sait qu'elles sont de bonne qualité dans ce magasin. Il (a demandé, est demandé) à sa cousine si elle pouvait lui montrer aussi des cravates. Lucienne (est descendue, est descendu) à la réserve et lui (a montré, est montrée) de belles cravates venues directement de Paris. "Est-ce que tu les aimes, André?", lui (a-t-elle demandé, a-t- elle demandée). Il (ne lui a pas répondu, ne lui est pas répondu) tout de suite car il ne voulait pas payer trop cher.*

> *Lucienne travaille dans une chemiserie. Là elle vend naturellement des chemises. Elle faisait même les étalages. Son cousin André **est venu** et **a acheté** des chemises pour son travail de bureau. Il **les a prises** car il sait qu'elles sont de bonne qualité dans ce magasin. Il **a demandé** à sa cousine si elle pouvait lui montrer aussi des cravates. Lucienne **est descendue** à la réserve et lui **a montré** de belles cravates venues directement de Paris. "Est-ce que tu les aimes, André?", lui **a-t-elle demandé**. Il **ne lui a pas répondu** tout de suite car il ne voulait pas payer trop cher.*

Est venu is correct because verbs that deal with motion take the auxiliary verb *être. A acheté* is correct because there is no agreement in the participle when the object comes after the verb. *Les a prises* is correct in the next sentence because the direct object precedes the verb and there must be agreement with *les* which stands for *chemises*, a plural feminine word. *A demandé* is a regular *passé composé* form with *avoir. Est descendue* is correct because in the *passé composé* verbs with *être* should show agreement with the noun. *Descendue* must be feminine because it refers to *Lucienne. A montré* is a regular *passé composé* verb with *avoir* in which there is no agreement. *A-t-elle demandé* and *lui a répondu* are both regular and take *avoir*, so there should be no agreement.

8.4 L'imparfait

The term **"imperfect"** signifies **"not perfected or finished"** and this attribute distinguishes it from the *passé composé*. Unlike the *passé composé,* it is a simple form (with no auxiliary).

8.4.1 Formation

Take the *nous* form of the present tense; remove the ending *–ons.* To the remaining stem add: *–ais, –ais, –ait, –ions, –iez, –aient.*

Exception: *être: j'étais, tu étais, il était, nous étions, vous étiez, ils étaient.*

Je dansais. I danced, I used to dance, I was dancing.

Donner: *je donnais*	**Finir:** *je finissais*
Écrire: *j'écrivais*	**Étudier:** *j'étudiais, nous étudiions*
Manger: *je mangeais*	**Commencer:** *je commençais*
Préférer: *je préférais*	**Appeler:** *j'appelais*

8.4.2 Usage

Unlike the *passé composé,* which denotes **an action completed within a specified or implied time frame,** the imperfect is a tense of **description, condition, repetition,** or **habitual action.** This time frame can also be prolonged when using the *imparfait* for a repeated, habitual, or routine action in the past. For example: *Tous les matins, je me promenais au bord de la mer.* Every morning I used to (I would) go for a walk by the ocean.

> *Quand j'étais jeune, je faisais beaucoup de sport.* [General description of habitual, repeated action.] When I was young, I played a lot of sports.

> *Puisque Marc avait mal au dos, il ne pouvait pas marcher vite.* [Description of physical/mental condition.] Since Marc had a backache, he couldn't walk fast.

> *Le ciel était bleu, le vent touchait légèrement le bout des fleurs, qui semblaient heureuses. Il faisait très beau et nous avions envie de rester au jardin mais il fallait rentrer dans la maison.* The sky was blue, the wind lightly touched the edges of the flowers, which seemed to be happy. It was a beautiful day and we felt like staying in the garden, but we had to go inside the house. [As you can see, an entire passage may be expressed in the imperfect, if it involves description of the weather, the décor, mental and/or physical conditions, i.e., "how things were."]

8.4.3 *Quand*

Two **simultaneous actions** that took place in the past may be expressed by the imperfect using *quand.*

> *Quand nous parlions, elle regardait la télé.* When we were speaking, she was watching TV.

> *Claudette avait cinq ans quand son père travaillait à Nice.* Claudette was five years old when her father was working in Nice.

> *Quand tu entrais, nous sortions.* When you were coming in, we were going out.

ATTENTION:

> *Robert ne savait pas quand son cousin allait revenir.* Robert didn't know when his cousin was going to return.

Note: *Aller* is **always** used in the **imperfect** as an auxiliary to express the future in the past ("was going to do something").

Problem Solving Example:

Rewrite the following sentences in the *imparfait*.

1. *Je suis un étudiant en mathématiques.*
2. *Elle habite rue de la Rochelle.*
3. *Vous dînez souvent au restaurant.*
4. *Ils ont peur de leurs profs.*
5. *Tu fais du progrès.*

1. *J'étais un étudiant en mathématiques.*
2. *Elle **habitait** rue de la Rochelle.*
3. *Vous **diniez** souvent au restaurant.*
4. *Ils **avaient** peur de leurs profs.*
5. *Tu **faisais** du progrès.*

8.4.4 *L'imparfait* versus *le Passé Composé*

Although theoretically any verb may be used in any tense, some verbs are used **almost exclusively** in the **imperfect** because of their meaning, e.g., *être, avoir, pouvoir, vouloir, savoir, aimer, détester, préférer,* etc., which describe conditions, states of mind, or emotions.

Under certain circumstances, these verbs may be used in the *passé composé* in order to isolate a particular moment or an extraordinary situation or event.

*Ce matin elle **a eu** mal à la tête à cause de son accident hier.* This morning she had a headache because of her accident yesterday. [The headache is gone now.]

*Le garçon regardait attentivement le film et tout à coup il **a pu** comprendre l'histoire.* The boy watched the movie carefully and all at once he could understand the story. [He succeeded in grasping it.]

*Le chat a vu le chien et soudain il **a voulu** courir.* The cat saw the dog and suddenly he tried to run. [The sense of *vouloir* is "to try" in this case.]

Hint: Key words like *tout à coup, soudain, immédiatement* often indicate the extraordinary circumstances that call for the use of the *passé composé* for these verbs.

Remember:

- Use the *imparfait* for description, condition, repetition, and habitual action.

- Certain verbs are used almost exclusively in the *imparfait* (*être, avoir, pouvoir, vouloir, savoir, aimer, détester, préferer,* etc.).

- The *passé composé* stands for an action completed in a specified or implied time. The *imparfait* is ongoing and has no indicated beginning or end.

Compare:

*Nous **écrivions** une carte postale quand le train **est arrivé**.* We were writing a postcard when the train arrived. [*Passé composé* interrupts the ongoing action of the imperfect.]

*Sophie **a ouvert** la boîte et elle **a ri** de plaisir.* Sophie opened the box and laughed with pleasure. [Two actions in the *passé composé*; one inspires the other. Both actions are completed within a specific time.]

*Sam **était** fatigué et il **ne voulait pas** manger.* Sam was tired and didn't want to eat. [Two descriptive actions, both imperfect because both have no indicated beginning or end.]

Problem Solving Example:

In the following passage, decide which past tense would be more appropriate by circling your choice.

*Mireille (**avait / a eu**) vingt ans quand elle (**arrivait / est arrivée**) à l'université pour la première fois. Elle (**était / a été**) étudiante, mais elle (**ne connaissait pas / n'a pas connu**) les autres étudiants. Quand elle (**entrait / est entrée**) dans sa chambre, une jeune fille y (**était / a été**) déjà. C' (**était / a été**) sa nouvelle camarade de chambre. Cet après-midi-là, elles (**sortaient / sont sorties**) pour*

*explorer un peu le campus. Il (**faisait** / **a fait**) beau, et les oiseaux (**chantaient** / **ont chanté**). Mireille et sa nouvelle amie (**étaient** / **ont été**) très heureuses. Elles (**allaient** / **sont allées**) à la librairie pour acheter leurs livres, et elles (**prenaient** / **ont pris**) des glaces après le dîner à la cafétéria. Ensuite, elles (**retournaient** / **sont retournées**) dans leur chambre à la résidence universitaire pour rencontrer d'autres étudiants.*

*Mireille **avait** vingt ans quand elle **est arrivée** à l'université pour la première fois. Elle **était** étudiante, mais elle **ne connaissait pas** les autres étudiants. Quand elle **est entrée** dans sa chambre, une jeune fille y **était** déjà. C' **était** sa nouvelle camarade de chambre. Cet après-midi-là, elles **sont sorties** pour explorer un peu le campus. Il **faisait** beau, et les oiseaux **chantaient**. Mireille et sa nouvelle amie **étaient** très heureuses. Elles **sont allées** à la librairie pour acheter leurs livres, et elles **ont pris** des glaces après le dîner à la cafétéria. Ensuite, elles **sont retournées** dans leur chambre à la résidence universitaire pour rencontrer d'autres étudiants.*

8.5   *Le Plus-que-parfait*

The **pluperfect** denotes something further away in the past. It is a compound tense that is used **to compare two past actions.** It may be used with the *passé composé* or the imperfect.

8.5.1 Formation

The imperfect form of *avoir* or *être* is used as an **auxiliary** with the **past participle.** The same rules of **agreement** that apply to the *passé composé* govern the *plus-que-parfait.*

*Hier j'ai reçu la lettre que Jean **avait envoyée** il y a trois semaines.*
Yesterday I received the letter that Jean (had) sent three weeks ago. [The action of sending the letter precedes its receipt. Both actions are in the past.]

*Gigi **était déjà arrivée** quand **nous avons téléphoné**.* Gigi had already arrived when we phoned.

*Philippe **oubliait** toujours le nom des gens qu'il **avait rencontrés**.* Philippe always used to forget the names of people he (had) met.

Problem Solving Example:

In the following sentences, use the *plus-que-parfait* (the pluperfect). Be sure to place adverbs in their proper locations.

1. *Je portais la chemise que tu _____ (**acheter**).*
2. *J'allais inviter mes amis à ta fête, mais Jeanne _____ (**déjà téléphoner**) à tout le monde.*
3. *Marianne a pu se coucher tôt parce qu'elle _____ (**si bien faire**) sa valise à l'avance.*
4. *Nous _____ (**déjà arriver**) quand vous êtes partis.*
5. *Je _____ (**déjà terminer**) mes devoirs quand la cloche a sonné.*

1. *Je portais la chemise que tu **avais achetée**.*
2. *J'allais inviter mes amis à ta fête, mais Jeanne **avait déjà téléphoné** à tout le monde.*
3. *Marianne a pu se coucher tôt parce qu'elle **avait** si bien **fait** sa valise à l'avance.*
4. *Nous **étions** déjà **arrivés** quand vous êtes partis.*
5. *J'**avais** déjà **terminé** mes devoirs quand la cloche a sonné.*

8.6 Le Futur Proche

Le futur proche (the near future) is a way of expressing actions that are going to be done in the future. In fact, in English, the *futur proche* means "to be going to do something." It is formed by using *aller* in the present tense (as an auxiliary) and the infinitive.

*Nous **allons voir** le nouvel ami de Laure ce soir.* We're going to see Laure's new friend this evening.

***Vas-tu payer** cette facture?* Are you going to pay this bill?

*L'année prochaine **ils ne vont pas visiter** le Midi.* Next year they're not going to visit the south of France.

Problem Solving Example:

Use the *futur proche* (the near future) to express the following ideas.
1. *Je mange à 6h.*
2. *Nous dansons à la boîte Queen ce soir.*
3. *Elise rend visite à ses amies.*
4. *Je suis en retard.*
5. *Vous avez des dettes.*
6. *Tu fais du progrès en français.*
7. *Diane et Pluto se disputent.*

1. *Je **vais manger** à 6h.*
2. *Nous **allons danser** à la boîte Queen ce soir.*
3. *Elise **va rendre** visite à ses amies.*
4. *Je **vais être** en retard.*
5. *Vous **allez avoir** des dettes.*
6. *Tu **vas faire** du progrès en français.*
7. *Diane et Pluto **vont se disputer.***

8.7 *Le Futur*

This tense expresses an action that is going to happen in the future. It is a simple tense (unlike the *futur proche,* which is a compound tense). In English the future is indicated by the words "will" or "shall."

8.7.1 Formation of Future Tense for Regular Verbs

The *futur* is based on the infinitive. To form a future verb, simply add the appropriate ending *–ai, –as, –a, –ons, –ez, –ont* to the infinitive of the verb.

–ar verb	*–ir* verb	*–re* verb
je parlerai	*je finirai*	*je vendrai*
tu parleras	*tu finiras*	*tu vendras*

il parlera	il finira	il vendra
elle parlera	elle finira	elle vendra
nous parlerons	nous finirons	nous vendrons
vous parlerez	vous finirez	vous vendrez
ils parleront	ils finiront	ils vendront
elles parleront	elles finiront	elles vendront

8.7.2 Common Irregular Verbs

Stems change; endings do not.

avoir: j'**aur**ai	être: je **ser**ai	faire: je **fer**ai
aller: j'**ir**ai	dire: je **dir**ai	venir: je **viendr**ai
courir: je **courr**ai	pouvoir: je **pourr**ai	vouloir: je **voudr**ai
savoir: je **saur**ai	essayer: j'**essaier**ai	voir: je **verr**ai

Quand je serai à Paris, j'irai le voir. When I'm in Paris, I'll go see him.

Je ne sais pas quand elle partira. I don't know when she's leaving.

Note: When *"quand"* is followed by a **future action,** the verb must be in the **future,** even though in English we often translate it in the present.

Problem Solving Example:

Respond to the following questions in the *futur.*

1. *Je vais à la banque aujourd'hui. Et la semaine prochaine?*
2. *Il fait beau aujourd'hui. Et demain?*
3. *Nous nous couchons tard d'habitude. Et ce soir?*
4. *Vous rendez visite à la famille Clinton en ce moment. Et l'année prochaine?*
5. *Je peux manger n'importe quoi maintenant. Et quand je serai plus âgé(e)?*

1. *La semaine prochaine, j'**irai** à la banque.*
2. *Demain, il **fera** beau.*
3. *Ce soir, nous nous **coucherons** tard.*

4. *L'année prochaine, vous **rendrez visite** à la famille Clinton.*

5. *Quand je serai plus âgé(e), je **pourrai** manger n'importe quoi.*

8.8 Le Conditionnel

The conditional is a **mood** (with a present and past tense) that is always based on a **hypothetical situation** ("if" certain circumstances occur, "then" . . .). The "if" may be expressed or implied.

8.8.1 Formation

Like the future, the conditional uses the **infinitive** as its stem. To form the conditional, add the appropriate ending: *–ais, –ais, –ait, –ions, –iez, –aient* to the infinitive. Irregular conditional verbs use the same stems as irregular future verbs.

je parlerais	*je finirais*	*je vendrais*
nous parlerions	*nous finirions*	*nous vendrions*
ils parleraient	*ils finiraient*	*ils vendraient*

Hint: There is always an "r" in the conditional to differentiate it from the imperfect, which has the same endings.

Imperfect	Conditional	Imperfect	Conditional
je dansais	*je danserais*	*je voulais*	*je voudrais*
je venais	*je viendrais*	*j'étais*	*je serais*
j'avais	*j'aurais*	*je faisais*	*je ferais*
je voyais	*je verrais*	*je finissais*	*je finirais*
je pouvais	*je pourrais*		

*Sans son aide, nous ne **saurions** pas utiliser cette machine.* Without his help, we wouldn't know how to use this machine.

*Pauline **serait** ravie de recevoir ce livre.* Pauline would be delighted to receive this book.

*Je **viendrais** te parler ce soir.* I'd come to talk to you tonight.

*Daniel **voudrait** du poisson et de la salade.* Daniel would like some fish and salad. [The conditional of ***vouloir*** is used for politeness instead of the present of the indicative *je veux*.]

Problem Solving Example:

Rewrite the following sentences in the conditional mood.

1. *Je m'habille rapidement.*
2. *Tu oublies qui est le prof.*
3. *Vous rencontrez plein de gens ici.*
4. *Elle est fâchée.*
5. *Stéphane et Guillaume veulent du café.*
6. *Nous aimons manger tout de suite.*

1. *Je m'**habillerais** rapidement.*
2. *Tu **oublierais** qui est le prof.*
3. *Vous **rencontreriez** plein de gens ici.*
4. *Elle **serait** fâchée.*
5. *Stéphane et Guillaume **voudraient** du café.*
6. *Nous **aimerions** manger tout de suite.*

8.8.2 The Past Conditional

The past conditional is further away in possibility and time, and often expresses regret.

Formation: The conditional of *avoir* or *être* + **past participle.**

*J'**aurais voulu** le voir.* I would have liked to see him.

*Elle **serait allée** avec toi.* She would have gone with you.

*Nous **ne** leur **aurions pas raconté** cette histoire.* We wouldn't have told them that story.

8.8.3 The Future and Conditional with "If" Clauses

If . . .	Result . . .
Present: *Si j'ai le temps*	Future: *j'irai chez lui.*
Imperfect: *Si j'avais le temps*	Conditional: *j'irais chez lui.*
Pluperfect: *Si j'avais eu le temps*	Past Conditional: *je serais allé*

These structures correspond to English: If I **have** the time, **I'll do** it; If I **had** the time, I **would do** it; If I **had had** the time, I **would have done** it.

Problem Solving Examples:

Use either a **future** form or a **conditional** form for the verbs in the sentences below. The **infinitive** is given in capital letters for your reference.

> *Ce soir nous **ALLER VOIR** le nouveau bébé de Simone. **VENIR**-vous aussi? Au cas où vous ne **POUVOIR** vous libérer, je **PARLER** à Simone pour changer la visite. Je **VOULOIR** pouvoir vous prévenir à l'avance mais nous avons décidé de cette visite à la dernière minute.*

> *Ce soir nous **allons voir** le nouveau bébé de Simone. **Viendrez**-vous aussi? Au cas où vous ne **pourrez** vous libérer, je **parlerai** à Simone pour changer la visite. **J'aurais voulu** pouvoir vous prévenir à l'avance mais nous avons décidé de cette visite à la dernière minute.*

The first verb in the sentence is in the *futur proche*. The second verb is in the *futur*. The third verb is expressing doubt, therefore the *conditionne* is used. The fourth verb shows certainty, so the *futur* is used. The last verb shows a possibility further away in time so the *conditionne passé* is used.

In the following sentences, decide if the missing verb should be in (1) the conditional mood or the imperfect tense, (2) the present or future tense, or (3) the pluperfect tense or the past conditional mood.

1. *Si j'avais des millions de dollars, je _____ (être) heureux/ heureuse.*
2. *Je serais allé à la banque si je _____ (avoir) assez d'argent.*
3. *Si je suis en forme, je _____ (aller) au gymnase.*
4. *Je danserais toute la nuit si je _____ (être) en vacances.*
5. *Si je _____ (sortir), je verrai mes amis.*

6. *Vous _____ (avoir) plus d'argent si vous sortiez moins.*

1. *serais (conditional)*
2. *avais eu (pluperfect)*
3. *irai (future)*
4. *étais (imperfect)*
5. *sors (present)*
6. *auriez (conditional)*

8.9 L'infinitif

When two present tense verbs are used together, the **second verb** is always in the **infinitive.** The following verbs are followed **directly** by the infinitive with **no preposition:**

*Nous **aimons** danser.* We like to dance.

*Ils ne **savent** pas lire.* They don't know how to read.

*Margot **déteste** travailler.* Margot hates to work.

*Cet homme **adore** manger.* This man loves to eat.

8.9.1 As a Noun

The infinitive may also be used as a noun, as the subject or object of the sentence, or as the object of a preposition:

*Bien **dormir** est très important.* Sleeping well is very important.

8.9.2 L'infinitif Passé

L'infinitif passé uses *avoir* or *être* as the **auxiliary + the past participle** (*après avoir vu; après être venu*) to express "after having done something." *Avant de* + **the infinitive** (*avant de voir; avant de venir*) is used for "before doing something."

> ***Avant de faire** son lit, Marie a cherché des draps.* Before making her bed, Marie looked for some sheets.
>
> *Jacques prépare son dîner **après avoir étudié.*** Jacques makes his dinner after having studied.

*Elle nous a vus **après être rentrée**.* After coming home, she saw us.

__Après être tombée__, Suzy a ri. After falling down, Suzy laughed.

*Il nous écrira **avant de partir**.* He'll write to us before he leaves.

Note: **One subject** performs **both actions**. The participle agrees with the **subject** with *être* and with the **preceding direct object** with *avoir*. The verb in the second action may be in the present, past, or future tense.

Problem Solving Example:

Choose the correct word from the choices in parentheses below:

> *Ce soir, Camille est allée au cinéma. Elle a decidé de sortir après (**avoir fini, finit**) ses devoirs. Elle a diné avant de (**partir, avoir parti**) parce qu'elle avait faim. Après être (**revenu, revenue**) elle était fatiguée. Avant de (**s'est endormie, s'endormir**) elle a téléphoné son ami.*

> *Ce soir, Camille est allée au cinéma. Elle a decidé de sortir après **avoir fini** ses devoirs. Elle a diné avant de **partir** parce qu'elle avait faim. Après être **revenue** elle était fatiguée. Avant de **s'endormir** elle a téléphoné son ami.*

Remember that an infinitive must follow *avant de* and a participle must follow *après avoir* or *après être*. There is agreement with the subject when *être* is the auxiliary verb of this construction.

8.10 *Le Participe Présent*

The present participle is formed by adding *–ant* to the stem of the *nous* form of the present:

parlant, finissant, rompant. **Exceptions:** *étant, ayant, sachant.*

8.10.1 As an Adjective

The present participle may act as an **adjective:**

"L'homme est un roseau pensant." (Pascal) "Man is a thinking reed."

8.10.2 With *En*

The **only** preposition used with the present participle is *en* ("by," "while," or "upon" doing something):

En fermant la porte, il a laissé son chat dehors. By closing the door, he left his cat outside.

Le vieillard est mort heureux en sachant la vérité. The old man died happy, upon learning the truth.

Elle peut chanter en dansant. She can sing while dancing.

Note: The **same subject** performs both actions.

8.11 *Les Verbes Pronominaux*

As the name implies, pronominal verbs are always accompanied by a **pronoun** *(me, te, se, nous, vous, se)*. They are used in **reciprocal, reflexive,** and **idiomatic** constructions.

8.11.1 Reciprocal

Reciprocal verbs indicate a reciprocal action between two parties. They are usually translated with the English expression "each other."

Roméo et Juliette s'aiment. Romeo and Juliet **love each other.**

Nous nous écrivons chaque mois. We **write to each other** every month. [The first *nous* is subject; the second is the indirect object pronoun.]

Vous vous regardez longtemps. You **look at each other** for a long time.

Ils se voient tous les jours. They **see each other** every day.

8.11.2 Reflexive

Reflexive verbs indicate that the action of the verbs fall on the subject. It corresponds to the English expressions "to do something to oneself" or "to do something for oneself." The auxiliary verb for every pronominal verb in a compound tense, such as the *passé composé*, is *être*.

Bette se lave. Bette washes herself.

Bette se lave les mains. Bette washes her hands (for herself).

Bette s'est lavé les mains. Bette washed her hands (for herself).

With reflexive verbs, follow the rule of agreement for *être* (participle agrees with the subject) unless there is a direct object preceding the verb. In that case, follow the rule of *avoir* (participle agrees with object).

Bette s'est lavée. Bette washed herself.

Bette se les est lavées. Bette washed them (for herself).

Note that the direct object *les* now precedes the verb. Therefore, agreement is made with *les*, which refers to *mains*, a feminine plural noun.

Problem Solving Example:

Q Fill in the following blanks with the correct usage of the pronominal verbs indicated in parentheses.

1. *(se reposer) Quand on est fatigué, il faut qu'on* _____.
2. *(se brosser les dents) Hier, avant de me coucher, je* _____.
3. *(se dépêcher) Jacques est en retard, il doit* _____.
4. *(se trouver) La Tour Eiffel* _____ *à Paris.*
5. *(s'intéresser à) Ce petit* _____ *toutes les jeunes filles.*
6. *(s'amuser) Est-ce que vous* _____ *ensemble?*
7. *(se coucher) Nous* _____ *avant minuit . . . il le faut!*
8. *(se raser) Lundi passé, je* _____ *la barbe. Je me la suis* _____ .
9. *(s'habiller) Maman* _____ *lentement.*
10. *(se moquer de) Les enfants* _____ *leur prof M. Méchant.*

1. *Quand on est fatigué, il faut qu'on se repose.*
2. *Hier, avant de me coucher, je me **suis brossé les dents**.*
3. *Jacques est en retard, il doit se **dépêcher**.*
4. *La Tour Eiffel se **trouve** à Paris.*
5. *Ce petit s'**intéresse** à toutes les jeunes filles.*
6. *Est-ce que vous **vous amusez** ensemble?*
7. *Nous **nous couchons** avant minuit . . . il le faut!*
8. *Lundi passé, je me **suis rasé** la barbe. Je me la **suis rasée**.*
9. *Maman s'**habille** lentement.*
10. *Les enfants se **moquent** de leur prof M. Méchant.*

8.11.3 Common Idiomatic Use of Pronominal Verbs

To express the **passive voice** (i.e., the action falls on the subject instead of an object), the **reflexive form** is often used:

Le français se parle au Canada. French is spoken in Canada.

Monsieur, cela ne se fait pas ici! Sir, that isn't done here!

Les journaux se vendent au kiosque. Papers are sold at the kiosk.

Note: The verb agrees in number with the subject.

8.12 Two Other Past Tenses of the Indicative

Two other past tenses of the indicative are *le passé simple* and *le passé antérieur*. Both of these tenses are used in writing, rather than in conversation. (Many modern writers use the *passé composé, imparfait,* and *plus-que-parfait* instead of these tenses.)

Le passé simple (historic or literary past) describes an action finished at a well-defined moment in the past.

Formation of regular verbs: Add to the stem the following endings:

–er verbs	*–ir* verbs	*–re* verbs
je parlai	*je finis*	*je vendis*
tu parlas	*tu finis*	*tu vendis*
il parla	*il finit*	*il vendit*

nous parlâmes	*nous finîmes*	*nous vendîmes*
vous parlâtes	*vous finîtes*	*vous vendîtes*
ils parlèrent	*ils finirent*	*ils vendirent*

*Napoléon **entra** dans la salle et **prit** son épée.* Napoleon entered the room and took his sword.

*Les princes **rendirent** le terrain aux paysans.* The princes gave back the land to the peasants.

8.12.1 Some Irregular Forms of the *Passé Simple*

avoir: j'eus	*être: je fus*	*savoir: je sus*
faire: je fis	*pouvoir: je pus*	*connaître: je connus*
écrire: j'écrivis	*vouloir: je voulus*	*falloir: il fallut*
lire: je lus	*voir: je vis*	*craindre: je craignis*

8.12.2 *Le Passé Antérieur*

Le *passé antérieur*, another literary tense, is used to show action that **immediately precedes** the *passé simple*. (Their relationship is similar to that of the **plus-que-parfait** and the *passé composé*.)

Formation: Use the *passé simple* of *avoir* or *être* with the *past participle*:

*Quand ils **eurent trouvé** la maison, ils **frappèrent** à la porte.* When they (had) found the house, they knocked at the door.

*Marcel **arriva** aussitôt que son père **fut parti**.* Marcel arrived right after his father left.

CHAPTER 9

The Subjunctive

9.1 Rules of the Subjunctive

The subjunctive is a **mood** that communicates emotions, wishes, desires, opinions, doubts — the subjective state of mind — of one agent acting upon another. Certain factors must be present for its use:

1. there must be **two different** subjects in **two clauses: one main, one subordinate;**

2. the subordinate clause must be introduced by *que*;

3. an expression of emotion, doubt, necessity, etc. must be present in the main clause.

9.2 Formation: Regular Verbs

To form the subjunctive drop the *–er, –ir,* or *–re* ending of the regular verb and add the following subjunctive endings: *e, es, e, ions, iez, ent.*

–er verbs	*–ir* verbs	*–re* verbs
que je mange	*que je dorme*	*que je rende*
que tu manges	*que tu dormes*	*que tu rendes*
qu'il mange	*qu'il dorme*	*qu'il rende*
que nous mangions	*que nous dormions*	*que nous rendions*
que vous mangiez	*que vous dormiez*	*que vous rendiez*
qu'ils mangent	*qu'ils dorment*	*qu'ils rendent*

9.2.1 Formation: Irregular Verbs

Irregular verbs have the same endings as regular verbs, except their stems are irregular.

Some common irregular forms:

faire: que je fasse

dire: que je dise

pouvoir: que je puisse

mettre: que je mette

craindre: que je craigne

vivre: que je vive

savoir: que je sache

rire: que je rie, que nous riions

lire: que je lise

écrire: que j'écrive, que nous écrivions

prendre: que je prenne, que nous prenions, qu'ils prennent

vouloir: que je veuille, que nous voulions, qu'ils veuillent

aller: que j'aille, que nous allions, qu'ils aillent

venir: que je vienne, que nous venions, qu'ils viennent

voir: que je voie, que nous voyions, qu'ils voient

boire: que je boive, que nous buvions, qu'ils boivent

mourir: que je meure, que nous mourions, qu'ils meurent

devoir: que je doive, que nous devions, qu'ils doivent

recevoir: que je reçoive, que nous recevions, qu'ils reçoivent

Note:

être		*avoir*	
que tu sois	*que je sois*	*que tu aies*	*que j'aie*
qu'il soit	*que nous soyons*	*qu'il ait*	*que nous ayons*
que vous soyez	*qu'ils soient*	*que vous ayez*	*qu'ils aient*

9.3 Uses of the Subjunctive in Subordinate Clauses

When using the subjunctive in subordinate clauses:

With **expressions of necessity:**

> *Il faut que Pierre me **rende** cet argent.* Pierre must give that money back to me. (Or) It's necessary that Pierre give . . .

> *Est-ce qu'**il est nécessaire que** tu **ailles** chez tes parents?* Do you have to go to your parents' house?

> *Ses amis **exigent que** Diane leur **écrive** des lettres.* Her friends insist that Diane write them letters.

With **expressions of desire or will:**

> ***Voulez-vous que** nous **venions** à midi?* Do you want us to come at noon?

> *L'enfant **préfère que** sa mère lui **tienne** la main.* The child prefers that his mother hold his hand.

> *Nous **désirons que** la paix **soit** faite au monde.* We want peace to be made in the world.

> *Je **souhaite que** Marcel te **dise** la vérité.* I wish that Marcel would tell you the truth.

With **expressions of emotion:**

> *Laurent **n'aime pas que** tu **partes** si tôt.* Laurent doesn't like you to be leaving so soon.

> *Ils **ont peur que** cette voiture **ne puisse pas** faire le voyage.* They're afraid that this car can't make the trip.

> *Votre père **est heureux que** vous **compreniez** le problème.* Your father is glad that you understand the problem.

With **expressions of doubt:**

> ***Il est douteux que** nous **fassions** ce dîner.* It's doubtful that we'll make that dinner.

Je ne suis pas certaine que Jean *vienne* avec nous. I'm not sure Jean's coming with us.

Elle n'est pas convaincue que cette situation *soit* bonne. She's not convinced that this situation is a good one.

With **impersonal** expressions (that convey a **subjective** idea):

Il est important que tu *étudies* cette leçon. It's important that you study this lesson.

Il est temps que nous *nous en allions.* It's time for us to leave.

C'est dommage que tu ne *saches pas* son adresse. It's too bad you don't know her address.

Il est inutile que vous *vous dépêchiez.* It's useless for you to hurry.

Il est possible que cet homme *veuille* travailler ici. It's possible that this man wants to work here.

Note: When there is more **certainty** than doubt, the **indicative** is used:

Il est probable que nous *allons* à Marseille. We will probably go to Marseilles.

Elle est certaine que son mari *peut* réparer la télé. She's sure her husband can repair the TV.

On est sûr que les voisins *ont acheté* une nouvelle maison. We're sure the neighbors bought a new house.

With *espérer, penser,* and *croire:* When these verbs are **in the affirmative** ("I hope," "I think," "I believe"), the verb is in the **indicative:**

Vous espérez que leur avion *partira* à l'heure. You hope their plane will leave on time.

Je pense que Sylvie *est* très intelligente. I think Sylvie is very smart.

*Le petit **croit que** son père **va** jouer avec lui.* The child thinks his father will play with him.

However, when these verbs are either **negative** or **interrogative,** since there may be doubt involved, the **subjunctive** is used:

*Je **n'espère pas** qu'elle m'écrive.* I don't hope she'll write me.

***Pense-t-il que** sa cousine **revienne** bientôt?* Does he think his cousin will be back soon?

***Je ne crois pas** que Sara **puisse** nous accompagner.* I don't think Sara can go with us.

Problem Solving Example:

 Choose the correct form of the verb given in parentheses in the paragraph below.

*Dans la vie, il y a toujours beaucoup de choses que tout le monde (**fait, fasse**) tout simplement parce qu'il le faut. Il faut que nous (**faisons, fassions**) nos devoirs chaque soir, mais il est douteux que nous (**voulons, voulions**) faire les devoirs. C'est dommage que je ne (**peux, puisse**) pas lire or regarder la télé tout de suite après les devoirs, mais il faut d'abord que je (**mets, mette**) toute ma chambre bien en ordre et que (**je vais, j'aille**) m'inquiéter que personne n'a pas besoin de mes services. La vie (**est, soir**) vraiment compliquée.*

 *Dans la vie il y a toujours beaucoup de choses que tout le monde **fait** tout simplement parce qui'il le faut. Il faut que nous **fassions** nos devoirs chaque soir, mais il est douteux que nous **voulions** faire les devoirs. C'est dommage que je ne **puisse** pas lire ou regarder la télé tout de suite après les devoirs, mais il faut d'abord que je **mette** toute ma chambre bien en ordre et que **j'aille** m'inquiéter que personne n'a pas besoin de mes services. La vie **est** vraiment compliquée.*

Fait is correct because this is a certain statement and does not need the subjunctive. *Fassions* is correct because the subjunctive is always used after expressions of necessity like *il faut*. *Voulions* is correct because the subjunctive is also used after expressions of doubt like *il est douteux*. The subjunctive is also used after impersonal expressions like *c'est dommage*. Therefore, *puisse* is correct. *Mette* and *j'aille* are correct because the subjunctive is used after *il faut*. *Est* is correct because this is a statement of certainty and the subjunctive is not needed.

In the following sentences, use the correct mood (subjunctive or indicative) of the verbs given in parentheses.

1. *Qu'est-ce que vous voulez que je _____ (faire)?*
2. *Nous désirons que tu _____ (venir) avec nous ce week-end.*
3. *Je pense que tu _____ (être) bête!*
4. *Maman souhaite que nous _____(dire) toujours la vérité.*
5. *Il est probable que nous _____ (aller) chez Jean-Pierre demain.*
6. *Je ne crois pas que Marc _____ (pouvoir) continuer ses études de danse.*
7. *Le prof exige que chaque étudiant _____ (prendre) son travail au sérieux.*
8. *Il est possible que Jacques _____ (vouloir) venir avec nous au cinéma.*

1. *Qu'est-ce que vous voulez que je **fasse**?*
2. *Nous désirons que tu **viennes** avec nous ce week-end.*
3. *Je pense que tu **es** bête!*
4. *Maman souhaite que nous **disions** toujours la vérité.*
5. *Il est probable que nous **allons** chez Jean-Pierre demain.*
6. *Je ne crois pas que Marc **puisse** continuer ses études de danse.*
7. *Le prof exige que chaque étudiant **prenne** son travail au sérieux.*
8. *Il est possible que Jacques **veuille** venir avec nous au cinéma.*

Sentences 1, 2, and 4 take the subjunctive because they all have expressions of desire or will. Sentence 3 takes the indicative because *penser* only takes the subjunctive when the verb is negative or interrogative. Sentence 5 also takes the indicative because there is more certainty than doubt. Sentence 6 takes the subjunctive because *croire* is negative. Sentence 7 takes the subjunctive because *exiger* is a verb of necessity. The subjunctive is also used in Sentence 8 because *il est possible* is an impersonal expression, and impersonal expressions take the subjunctive.

9.4 Uses of the Subjunctive after Certain Conjunctions

After certain conjunctions that convey a sense of doubt or fear, the subjunctive is required:

> ***Avant que** tu le **saches**, l'hiver arrivera.* Before you know it, winter will be here.

> ***Pourvu que** mes amis **voient** Robert, ils nous téléphoneront.* Provided that my friends see Robert, they'll call us.

9.4.1 Conjunctions and Prepositions

Many of these conjunctions have corresponding **prepositions** that are used when there is only **one subject:**

Conjunction (+ Subjunctive) (Two subjects)	Preposition (+ Infinitive) (One subject for both actions)
à condition que – provided that	*à condition de*
afin que – in order that	*afin de*
à moins que – unless	*à moins de*
avant que – before	*avant de*
de crainte que – for fear that	*de crainte de*
de peur que – for fear that	*de peur de*
pour que – so that	*pour*

> ***De crainte d'**oublier le rendez-vous, **j'ai écrit** la date.* For fear of forgetting the appointment, I wrote down the date. (one subject)

Avant de partir, viens nous voir. Before you leave, come see us. (one subject)

Elle achètera cette voiture, à condition d'avoir assez d'argent. She'll buy the car, provided that she has enough money. (one subject)

But:

Elle recevra cette voiture, à condition que sor père ait assez d'argent. She will receive the car, provided that her father has enough money. (two subjects)

9.4.2 Conjunctions with the Subjunctive

Some conjunctions do not have a prepositional equivalent and require the **subjunctive, even with one subject:**

bien que – although	*de sorte que* – so that
malgré que – despite the fact that	*pourvu que* – provided that
jusqu'à ce que – until	*quoique* – although

Bien qu'il dorme beaucoup, il est toujours fatigué. Although he sleeps a lot, he's always tired.

Elle attendra ici jusqu'à ce qu'elle apprenne le résultat. She'll wait here until she finds out the results.

Quoique Sam fasse de son mieux, il ne réussit pas. Although Sam is doing his best, he isn't succeeding.

Note: The form *quoi que* (two words meaning "whatever" or "no matter what") also takes the subjunctive:

Quoi que tu dises, on ne va pas te croire. No matter what you say, they won't believe you.

Problem Solving Examples:

In each of the following sentences, the subjunctive is used. Explain why the subjunctive is correct in each case.

1. *Nous désirons toujours que tout se fasse le plus vite possible.*

2. *Nous n'aimons pas que mon frère parte si tôt de chez nous tous les jours.*
3. *Il n'est pas certain que nous faissons cette reception.*

1. The subjunctive is used because *désirer* is used as an expression of desire or will.
2. The subjunctive is used because *aimer* is an expression of emotion.
3. The subjunctive is used because there is a lack of certainty that qualifies as an expression of doubt.

Fill in the following blanks with the correct mood (subjunctive or indicative) of the verbs in parentheses.

1. *Quoiqu'elle _____ (**pouvoir**) être gentille, elle préfère être méchante.*
2. *Les examens de maths sont faciles pourvu que vous _____ (**étudier**) beaucoup en avance.*
3. *Bien que ce _____ (**être**) un métier mal payé, Jacques veut être professeur.*
4. *Il est retourné vite de crainte de _____ (**rater**) le train.*

1. *Quoiqu'elle **puisse** être gentille, elle préfère être méchante.*
2. *Les examens de maths sont faciles pourvu que vous **étudiiez** beaucoup en avance.*
3. *Bien que ce **soit** un métier mal payé, Jacques veut être professeur.*
4. *Il est retourné vite de crainte de **rater** le train.*

9.5   *Le Passé du Subjonctif*

The **past subjunctive** is a comparative tense used to contrast **an action in one tense** (in the principal clause) with **an action that preceded it** (in the subordinate clause). The auxiliary *avoir* or *être,* in the **subjunctive form,** is used with the **past participle.**

*Nous **sommes contents** que nos amis **soient** enfin **arrivés.*** We're happy (now) that our friends finally arrived (before now).

*Est-ce que tu **étais surprise** que Jeanne **t'ait envoyé** l'argent?* Were you surprised (yesterday) that Jean had sent you the money?

*Maurice **n'a pas cru** que sa fille **soit née**.* Maurice didn't believe his daughter had already been born.

9.5.1 Agreement of Tenses (La Concordance des Temps)

When two actions (one of which calls for the subjunctive) take place at the same time or in rapid chronological order, the present subjunctive is used. This applies to two simultaneous actions in past contexts as well. (Remember that the past subjunctive is only used to contrast an action in the principal clause with an action in the subordinate clause that happened before it.)

*Monique **était heureuse** que Virginie **ne parte pas**.* Monique was happy that Virginie wasn't leaving.

*Il **a parlé** lentement **afin que** nous **puissions** le comprendre.* He spoke slowly so that we were able to understand him.

*Il **fallait que** les employés **fassent** attention au patron.* The employees had to pay attention to the boss.

*Je **voulais que** mes amis **suivent** l'autre route.* I wanted my friends to take the other route.

*Tout le monde **doute que** Jacques **revienne** demain.* Everyone doubts that Jacques is coming back tomorrow.

> ## Quiz: Verbs and The Subjunctive

1. Il fallait que les étudiants _____ les exercices.

    (A) fassent   (C) aient fait

    (B) font   (D) ont fait

2. Roberta _____ à huit heures moins dix.

    (A) arrivait   (C) a arrivé

    (B) est arrivée   (D) a arrivée

3. Le chef de service _____ le travail hier.

    (A) ont distribué   (C) a distribué

    (B) a distribuée   (D) distribuera

4. C'est le matin et on commence à travailler, mais à midi tout le monde _____.

    (A) avait fini   (C) eut fini

    (B) aura fini   (D) finira

5. Quoique nous _____ beaucoup, la classe est difficile.

    (A) étudions   (C) étudiions

    (B) avons étudié   (D) étudierons

6. Je me suis brossé les dents. Je me les suis _____.

    (A) brossé   (C) brossées

    (B) brossés   (D) brossée

7. _____ ouvrant la porte, j'ai trouvé la verité.

    (A) Avec   (C) En

    (B) Quand   (D) Par

8. Bien _____, c'est necessaire?

    (A) mangeant   (C) mange

    (B) manger   (D) mangé

9. Si j'avais faim, _____ .

    (A) j'ai mangé   (C) je vais manger

    (B) je mangeais   (D) je mangerais

10. Si j'aime cette voiture, _____ cette voiture.

    (A) j'ai acheté   (C) j'achetais

    (B) j'acheterai   (D) j'acheterais

ANSWER KEY

1.	(A)	6.	(C)
2.	(B)	7.	(C)
3.	(C)	8.	(B)
4.	(B)	9.	(D)
5.	(C)	10.	(B)

CHAPTER 10

Adverbs

10.1 Formation of Adverbs

As in English, French adverbs modify verbs, adjectives, or other adverbs. There are adverbs of time, place, manner, quantity, negation, opinion, and adverbs that link ideas.

Many adverbs are formed by adding the suffix *–ment* (equivalent to the English suffix "–ly") to the **feminine** form of the adjective:

heureux	*heureuse*	*heureusement* (happily, luckily)
lent	*lente*	*lentement* (slowly)
doux	*douce*	*doucement* (softly, slowly, gently)
égal	*égale*	*également* (equally)
certain	*certaine*	*certainement* (certainly, surely)

10.1.1 Adjectives That End with Vowels

Adjectives that end in "e" or in **another vowel,** simply add *–ment:*

rapide	*rapidement*	*infini*	*infiniment*
sincère	*sincèrement*	*absolu*	*absolument*

10.2 Irregular Forms

(a) *Bien — mieux.*

(b) Adjectives that end in *–ant* and *–ent* form their adverbs by adding *–amment* or *–emment* as suffixes:

constant	*constamment*	*Elle chante **constamment**.* She sings constantly.
prudent	*prudemment*	*Nous avons agi **prudemment**.* We acted prudently (cautiously).
courant	*couramment*	*Parlent-ils **couramment**?* Do they speak fluently?

(c) Some adjectives form adverbs with the suffix *–ément*:

profond	*profondément*	*Nous avons été **profondément** émus.* We were deeply (profoundly) moved.
précis	*précisément*	*Vous avez reçu **précisément** ce que vous vouliez.* You received just what you wanted.
décidé	*décidément*	*C'était **décidément** sérieux.* It was decidedly (definitely) serious.
assuré	*assurément*	*Vous serez **assurément** à l'heure.* You'll surely be on time.

(d) ***bref – brièvement.*** *Il a parlé brièvement.* He spoke briefly.

(e) ***gentil – gentiment.*** *Elle m'a répondu gentiment.* She answered me politely.

Problem Solving Example:

Using the adjective given in capital letters, form and insert the appropriate adverb in the sentences of the paragraph below:

> *De loin je regardais Jean partir du pays. Il était triste. Il marchait **LENT** vers la gare où il allait **CERTAIN** prendre son train pour Paris. Il regrettait **SINCERE** de ne pas avoir pu rester plus longtemps en Normandie. Il avait **INFINI** envie de rebrousser (**means "go back"**) chemin. Étant donné que son père voulait qu'il aille étudier à Paris, il devait **ASSURÉ** se résigner au départ.*

*Il devra maintenant CONSTANT revenir REGULIER
en Normandie pour ne pas se sentir trop malheureux.*

*De loin je regardais Jean partir du pays. Il était triste. Il
marchait **lentement** vers la gare où il allait **certainement**
prendre son train pour Paris. Il regrettait **sincèrement** de
ne pas avoir pu rester plus longtemps en Normandie. Il
avait **infiniment** envie de rebrousser chemin. Étant donné
que son père voulait qu'il aille étudier à Paris, il devait
assurément se résigner au départ. Il devra maintenant
constamment revenir **régulièrement** en Normandie pour
ne pas se sentir trop malheureux.*

10.3 Placement of the Adverb

The adverb **precedes** an **adjective** or another **adverb**:

*Sam était **complètement** surpris.* Sam was completely surprised.

*Il m'a parlé **bien** sérieusement.* He spoke to me quite seriously.

10.3.1 With Simple Verbs

The adverb **follows** a simple verb:

*Nous le lui dirons **doucement**.* We'll tell him gently.

*Yves allait **souvent** chez eux.* Yves used to go to their house often.

10.3.2 With Compound Verbs

With a **compound** verb, the adverb **follows the auxiliary** (especially with short forms) or may **follow the participle** (with forms in
–ment):

*Simone est **presque** partie sans nous.* Simone nearly left without
us.

*Il a **toujours** aimé jouer.* He has always loved to play.

*Elle a **déjà** fini.* She finished already.

*Nous lui avons parlé **calmement**.* We spoke to her calmly.

*Ils sont entrés **bruyamment**.* They came in noisily.

Problem Solving Example:

Place the adverbs in parentheses into the sentences below in the correct grammatical position.

1. *(**toujours**) Mon mari et moi voulions conduire la voiture.*
2. *(**prudemment**) Ils ont conduit le camion.*
3. *(**précisément**) Mon fils aime conduire comme un fou.*
4. *(**déjà**) Est-ce que vous avez reçu votre permis de conduire?*

1. *Mon mari et moi voulions **toujours** conduire la voiture.*
2. *Ils ont conduit **prudemment** le camion.*
3. *Mon fils aime conduire **précisément** comme un fou.*
4. *Est-ce que vous avez **déjà** reçu votre permis de conduire?*

10.3.3 Adverbs of Time and Space

Place adverbs of time and space **after** the participle or at the **beginning** of the sentence:

***Hier** nous avons vu Charles.* We saw Charles yesterday.

*Le cheval est tombé **là-bas**.* The horse fell down over there.

*Vous m'avez **souvent** écrit **autrefois**.* You often wrote me in the past.

Note: *Souvent* (often), *déjà* (already), and *toujours* (always) are placed **before** the participle.

10.4 Comparative of Adverbs

As with adjectives, add ***aussi, plus,*** or ***moins*** for equal, superior, or inferior comparisons:

*Nous avons voyagé **aussi longtemps** qu'eux.* We traveled as long as they did.

*Jean écrit **plus correctement** que toi.* Jean writes more correctly than you.

*Sara nous parlait **moins librement** que Bette.* Sara spoke to us less freely than Bette did.

Hint: Remember that the comparative of *bien* is *mieux* (better) **without** *plus*. For **less well,** use *moins bien*:

*Angélique parle allemand **moins bien** que sa sœur.* Angelique speaks German worse than her sister.

*Sophie chante **mieux que** moi.* Sophie sings better than I do.

10.5 The Superlative

The superlative is formed by adding *le* to the comparative form and is **invariable:**

*Nancy danse **le plus gracieusement** de toute la famille.* Nancy dances the most gracefully of everyone in the family.

*C'est Philippe qui téléphone **le moins souvent**.* Phillip's the one who phones the least often.

10.6 Some Common Adverbs

Of quantity:

assez – enough	*très* – very
trop – too, too much	*tant* – so much
peu – little	

Of manner:

haut – high, loud	*bas* – low, quietly
vite – quickly	

Of time:

toujours – always, still	*jamais* – never
hier – yesterday	*aujourd'hui* – today
demain – tomorrow	*autrefois* – in the past

Of place:

ici – here	*là, là-bas* – there, over there
dehors – outside	*loin* – far

Of assent, dissent, and reasoning:

pourquoi – why, because	*ainsi* – thus
néanmoins – nevertheless	*pourtant* – however
cependant – however	*oui, non, peut-être* – yes, no, perhaps

Note: *peut-être* **is followed by** *que* **when it begins a sentence:**

Peut-être que *nous te verrons ce soir.* Perhaps we'll see you this evening.

10.7 Interrogative Adverbs

où – where	*quand* – when
comment – how	*pourquoi* – why
combien – how much, how many	

10.8 Adverbs That Connect Nouns, Phrases, and Clauses

d'abord – first, at first	*mais* – but
enfin – finally, at last	*ensuite* – next, then

D'abord *il ouvre la porte et* *ensuite* *il appelle son chien.* First he opens the door and then he calls his dog.

Problem Solving Example:

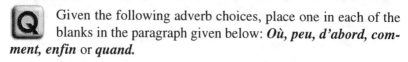

Given the following adverb choices, place one in each of the blanks in the paragraph given below: *Où, peu, d'abord, comment, enfin* or *quand.*

_____ *voulez-vois que Martine aille à cette heure avancée de la nuit?* _____ *et* _____ *pourrait-elle expliquer son absence?* _____ *il faudrait qu'elle puisse sortir de chez elle sans faire de bruit, mais le chien se chargerait bien d'aboyer! _____, ça n'a que très _____ d'importance puisqu'elle a décidé de ne pas sortir.*

*Où voulez-vous que Martine aille à cette heure avancée de la nuit? **Comment** et **quand** pourrait-elle expliquer son absence? **D'abord** il faudrait qu'elle puisse sortir de chez elle sans faire de bruit, mais le chien so chargerait biend d'aboyer! **Enfin** ça n'a que très **peu** d'importance puisqu'elle a décidé de ne pas sortir.*

CHAPTER 11

Prepositions and Conjunctions

11.1 Prepositions

A preposition introduces a phrase and has a noun, pronoun, or infinitive as its **object.** Prepositions are invariable.

Simple Prepositions:

avec – with	*sans* – without	*dans* – in
sur – on	*pour* – for	*par* – by
sous – under	*de* – of, from	*devant* – in front of
à – at, to	*derrière* – behind	*en* – in
contre – against	*entre* – between	*avant* – before (in time)

parmi – among (more than two things). *C'est **parmi** mes papiers.*
It's among my papers.

après – after (in time and space). *Viens **après** cinq heures.* Come
after 5 o'clock. *Il est arrivé **après** moi.* He arrived after me.

11.2 Compound Prepositions

Compound prepositions are composed of more than one word:

à côté de – next to	*autour de* – around (in space)
près de – near	*loin de* – far from

au-dessous de – underneath   *le long de* – along
en haut de – at the top of   *en bas de* – below
en face de – opposite   *à droite de* – to the right of
à gauche de – to the left of   *au-dessus de* – above
au milieu de – in the middle of   *jusqu'à* – until (in time and
space)

Problem Solving Example:

Fill in the blanks with the correct prepositions and conjunctions:

> *Elle est partie _____ lui _____ que ses amis se réveillent.*
> *_____ nous, je crois qu'elle est mal élevée.*

> *Elle est partie **avec** lui **avant** que ses amis se réveillent.*
> ***Entre** nous, je crois qu'elle est mal élevée.*

Avec means "with." *Avant* means "before." *Entre* means "between" and, with *nous*, is an idiomatic expression meaning "between us."

11.3 Prepositions with Geographic Names

For **cities,** always use *à:*

Je vais à Nice. I'm going to Nice.

Ils habitent à Chicago. They live in Chicago.

Allez-vous à Rome? Are you going to Rome?

Nous arriverons à Québec. We'll arrive in Quebec City.

Note: A few cities have an **article** in their name:

On s'arrête au Havre et à la Nouvelle Orléans. We're stopping at Le Havre and New Orleans.

For **large islands,** use *à:*

Ils sont à Hawaii. Elles sont à Cuba. They are in Hawaii. They are in Cuba.

For **"feminine" states, provinces, countries** or **continents** (those that end in an "e") use *en:*

> *Ils ont habité en Californie, en Floride, en France, en Allemagne, en Espagne, en Angleterre, en Afrique, en Europe, en Asie, en Italie, en Bretagne et en Provence.*

For **"masculine" countries** (those not ending in *"e"*) use *au*:

> *Je vais au Japon, au Portugal, au Canada, au Pérou.*

> *Je reviens du Danemark, du Congo, du Brésil, du Maroc, des États-Unis.*

Exceptions: *au Mexique; en Israël*

For the **names of states in the U.S.,** the same rule applies:

> *Nous voyageons en Californie, en Pennsylvanie, en Floride et en Virginie.*

> *Nous voyageons au Texas, au Missouri, au New Jersey et au Kansas.*

Note: A good "rule of thumb" is to use *dans l'état de . . .* + **the name of the state** when you're not sure of its gender:

> *Il pleut beaucoup dans l'état de Nebraska, de Michigan, d'Indiana, de North Dakota, etc.*

Problem Solving Example:

Fill in the blanks with the correct prepositions and conjunctions:

> *Monique préfère être _____ _____ hublot _____ avion. Elle va être _____ _____ sa maison. Je crois qu'elle va aller _____ Etats-Unis.*

> *Monique préfère être **près du** hublot **en** avion. Elle va être **loin de** sa maison. Je crois qu'elle va aller **aux** Etats-Unis.*

Près de is a compound preposition meaning "next to." *En* means "in." *Loin de* is a compound preposition meaning "far from." *Aux* is a plural masculine preposition describing the masculine noun *Etats-Unis* (United States).

11.4 Common Verbs + Preposition + Infinitive

11.4.1 Verb + *à*

When an infinitive follows certain verbs, the preposition *à* is used. These verbs include *aider à, commencer à, hesiter à, inviter à, se mettre à, rèussir à*, etc.

J'aide ma mère à faire le dîner. I help my mother make dinner.

Elle a commencé à danser. She started to dance.

Nous hésitons à le dire. We hesitate to say it.

On invite le professeur à parler. We invite the professor to speak.

Il s'est mis à pleurer. He started to cry.

Ont-elles réussi à finir le travail? Did they succeed in completing the work?

11.4.2 Verb + *de*

Likewise, there are other verbs that take the preposition *de* when followed by an infinitive. They include *accepter de, choisir de, conseiller de, décider de, demander de, empêcher de*, etc.

Margot accepte de lui téléphoner. Margot agrees to call him.

Simon a choisi d'acheter cette maison. Simon chose to buy this house.

Je te conseille d'aller. I advise you to go.

Continues-tu de souffrir? Are you still suffering?

Note: The verb *continuer* can be used with either *à* or *de*.

Ils ont décidé de partir. They decided to leave.

*J'ai **demandé à** Anne **de** m'écrire.* I asked Anne to write to me.

*Il m'**empêche de** parler.* He prevents me from speaking.

Note: See Chapter 12 for discussion of the verb ***manquer.***

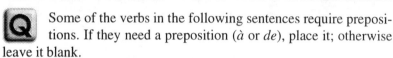

Problem Solving Example:

Some of the verbs in the following sentences require prepositions. If they need a preposition (*à* or *de*), place it; otherwise leave it blank.

1. *Je n'accepte pas _____ aller avec lui.*
2. *Maman hésite _____ ennuyer Papa parce qu'il se fâche facilement.*
3. *Monique vient _____ voir ses amies.*
4. *Le prof veut _____ nous donner des examens tous les jours.*
5. *Le bébé s'est mis _____ pleurer quand la cloche a sonné.*
6. *M. Téton m'a conseillé _____ rentrer tout de suite.*
7. *J'ai demandé au prof _____ m'écrire.*
8. *Paul a commencé _____ écrire sa thèse.*
9. *Les enfants aident leur mère _____ préparer la cuisine.*
10. *Mes parents ont décidé _____ partir.*

1. *Je n'accepte pas **d'** aller avec lui.*
2. *Maman hésite **à** ennuyer Papa parce qu'il se fâche facilement.*
3. *Monique vient **de** voir ses amies.*
4. *Le prof veut nous donner des examens tous les jours. (**no preposition needed**)*
5. *Le bébé s'est mis **à** pleurer quand la cloche a sonné.*
6. *M. Téton m'a conseillé **de** rentrer tout de suite.*
7. *J'ai demandé au prof **de** m'écrire.*
8. *Paul a commencé **à** écrire sa thèse.*
9. *Les enfants aident leur mère **à** préparer la cuisine.*
10. *Mes parents ont décidé **de** partir.*

11.5 Conjunctions

Conjunctions join words, phrases, or clauses. **Compound conjunctions** are followed by a clause.

Commonly used **simple conjunctions** include:

et – and	*mais* – but	*ou* – or
car – because	*donc* – thus, so	*comme* – as, since
quand – when	*lorsque* – when	*or* – well, so

Commonly used **compound conjunctions** include:

parce que – because	*dès que* – as soon as
alors que – while	*puisque* – since

Problem Solving Example:

Fill in the blanks with the correct conjunctions:

J'aide ma mère _____ _____ *le ménage* _____ *mon père est très malade. J'accepte* _____ *le faire.*

*J'aide ma mère **à faire** le ménage **car** mon père est très malade. J'accepte **de** le faire.*

A faire is used as the preposition + infinitive (to do). *Car* is a simple conjunction meaning "because" (*parce que* is a compound conjunction meaning "because," which may also be used here). Certain verbs require certain prepositions, for example, *accepter*, the verb, takes *de*.

Quiz: Adverbs & Prepositions and Conjunctions

1. J'ai dix-huit ans. Je viens _____ commencer mes études à l'université.

    (A) par   (C) à

    (B) au   (D) de

2. S'il vous plaît, envoyez la lettre _____ il est possible.

    (A) parce qu'   (C) puisqu'

    (B) dès qu'   (D) donc

3. Quand est-ce que vous arriverez _____ Québec?

    (A) à   (C) à la

    (B) au   (D) en

4. Je ne le vois pas souvent. Il habite _____ Mexique.

    (A) en   (C) à la

    (B) au   (D) dans

5. Je dois quitter la maison très tôt chaque matin parce que j'habite _____ l'école.

    (A) en haut de   (C) loin de

    (B) au milieu de   (D) près de

6. _____ quel état est-ce que Marie habite?

    (A) En   (C) Au

    (B) Dans   (D) À la

7. Nous avons decidé _____ manger au restaurant.

    (A) pour   (C) au

    (B) à   (D) de

8. _____ est-ce que vous préférez aller, à la plage _____ à la campagne?

    (A) Où, où   (C) Où, ou

    (B) Ou, où   (D) Ou, ou

9. Je ne peux pas choisir _____ les trois couleurs.

    (A) parmi   (C) contre

    (B) pour   (D) sous

10. _____ la banque et l'hôtel, il y a un supermarché.

    (A) Parmi   (C) Sous

    (B) Entre   (D) Sans

ANSWER KEY

1.	(D)	6.	(B)
2.	(B)	7.	(D)
3.	(A)	8.	·(C)
4.	(B)	9.	(A)
5.	(C)	10.	(B)

CHAPTER 12

Basic Idiomatic

Expressions

12.1 Expressions with *Avoir*

An idiom cannot be translated literally.

Expression	Example
avoir besoin de	*J'ai besoin d'argent.* I need money.
avoir confiance en	*Il a confiance en toi.* He trusts you.
avoir peur de	*Elle a peur de Jean.* She's afraid of John.
avoir honte de	*Ils ont honte de cela.* They're ashamed of it.
avoir envie de	*Tu as envie de rire.* You feel like laughing.
avoir l'air + adj.	*Elle a l'air riche.* She seems to be rich.
avoir l'air de + nom.	*Jim a l'air d'un idiot.* Jim looks like a fool.
avoir l'air de + inf.	*Il a l'air de souffrir.* He seems to be suffering.
avoir lieu	*Le concert a eu lieu hier soir.* The concert took place last night.
avoir mal	*Elle a mal à la tête.* She has a headache.
avoir chaud	*Avez-vous chaud?* Are you warm?
avoir faim	*C'est midi; j'ai faim.* It's noon; I'm hungry.
avoir soif	*Bill a toujours soif.* Bill's always thirsty.
avoir froid	*Nous avons très froid.* We're very cold.
avoir raison	*Sa mère a raison.* Her mother is right.
avoir sommeil	*As-tu sommeil?* Are you sleepy?

Expression	Example
avoir tort	*Ils **ont eu tort**.* They were wrong.
avoir + ans = age	*Claire **a 22 ans**.* Claire is 22.
avoir + âge	*Quel **âge avez-vous**?* How old are you?
avoir beau	*Tu **as beau** insister.* It's no use insisting.
avoir à + inf.	*Nous **avons à le faire**.* We have to do it.
avoir du mal à + inf.	*Il **a du mal à lire**.* He has trouble reading.
en avoir à quelqu'un	*J'**en ai à Thomas**.* I've got it in for Thomas.
en avoir assez	*Sa femme **en a assez**.* His wife is fed up.
en avoir pour + time	*J'**en ai pour une heure**.* It will take me an hour.
il y a	*Il **y a** six livres ici.* There are six books here.
il y a + time	*Je l'ai vu **il y a un mois**.* I saw him a month ago.
	*Il **y a un an** que je l'ai vu.* It's a year since I saw him.
il n'y a pas de quoi	*Merci, madame. **Il n'y a pas de quoi**.* Thanks, madam. Don't mention it. [Often: **Pas de quoi**.]

12.2 Expressions with *Faire*

ça, cela fait + time:

*Cela **fait un an** que tu étudies.* You've been studying for a year.

Expression	Example
ça fait	*Arrête! **Ça fait mal**!* Stop! That hurts!
	*Ça te **fera** du bien.* It will do you good.
faire semblant de	*Il **fait semblant de** l'aimer.* He pretends to like it.
s'en faire	*Ne **vous en faites** pas!* Don't worry!
faire la connaissance	*Enchanté de **faire votre connaissance**.* I'm pleased to meet you.

Expression	Example
faire un voyage	*Ils **font beaucoup de voyages.*** They travel a lot.
faire une promenade	***Faites une promenade.*** Go for a walk.
faire le plein	*Je **fais** toujours **le plein.*** I always fill the gas tank.
faire de la fièvre	*Le bébé **a fait de la fièvre.*** The baby had a fever.
faire Paris-Nîmes	*Le TGV **fait Paris-Nîmes** en trois heures.* The TGV goes from Paris to Nimes in three hours.
faire les magasins	*Anne **faisait tous les magasins.*** Anne went to all the stores.
faire un rôle	*Il va **faire Roméo.*** He's going to play Romeo.
n'avoir que faire de	*Je **n'ai que faire de** tes promesses!* I don't need your promises!
faire attention	***Fais attention!*** Watch out! [Pay attention!]
faire face à quelque chose	*Irène **fait face à** tous ses problèmes.* Irene is dealing with all her problems.
faire partie de	*Ils **font partie du** club.* They belong to the club.
faire de son mieux	*As-tu **fait de ton mieux** à l'examen?* Did you do your best on the exam?
faire sa médecine	*Simone **fait sa médecine** à Nice.* Simone is studying medicine in Nice.
faire ses valises	***Faites vos valises!*** Pack your bags!
se faire à quelque chose	*Nous nous **faisons à la situation.*** We're getting used to the situation.

12.2.1 Faire causatif

The **subject causes someone else to do the action:**

*Il **se fait** construire une maison.* He's having a house built for himself.

*Elle **se fait** toujours remarquer.* She always makes people notice her.

*Nous **ferons** jouer cette musique.* We'll have that music played.

*Il s'est **fait faire** un complet.* He had a suit made for himself.

Ils ont fait lire l'histoire par l'enfant. They had the child read the story.

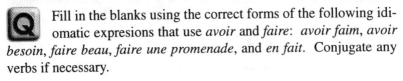

Problem Solving Example:

Fill in the blanks using the correct forms of the following idiomatic expresions that use *avoir* and *faire: avoir faim, avoir besoin, faire beau, faire une promenade,* and *en fait.* Conjugate any verbs if necessary.

> *Regardez le soleil! Qu'est-ce qu'il _____ aujourd'hui?*
> *Si on allait au parc? Voulez-vous _____ jusqu'au parc?*
> *Moi, je le veux bien. Ohh . . . mais j'_____ ; on peut avoir un pique-nique. Est-ce que cela vous tente?*
> *_____ , c'est une bonne idee! Il faut qu'on aille au supermarché parce que nous _____ de provisions pour le pique-nique.*

> *Regardez le soleil! Qu'est-ce qu'il **fait beau** aujourd'hui?*
> *Si on allait au parc? Voulez-vous **faire une promenade** jusqu'au parc? Moi, je le veux bien. Ohh . . . mais j'**ai faim**; on peut avoir un pique-nique. Est-ce que cela vous tente? **En fait,** c'est une bonne idee! Il faut qu'on aille au supermarché parce que nous **avons besoin** des provisions pour le pique-nique.*

12.3 Impersonal Expressions (with *il*)

Time:

Il est deux heures; il est minuit; il est trois heures moins le quart.
   [See Chapter 3 for a discussion of time.]

Il fait jour. It's daybreak.

Il fait nuit. Night is falling.

Il se fait tard. It's getting late.

Weather:

Il fait beau; mauvais; froid; chaud; lourd; frais. It's a beautiful day; nasty; cold; hot; humid; cool.

Il fait du soleil; des nuages; de la pluie; du brouillard. It's sunny; cloudy; rainy; foggy.

12.3.1 Other Idiomatic Expressions with *il*

Il s'agit de: it's a question of; it's a matter of; it deals with

Dans ce film, il s'agit de justice. This film is about (concerns itself with) justice.

Note: The verb *s'agir* is **only** conjugated in the third person masculine singular (like *falloir* = *il faut*).

Il s'agit de is usually prefaced by *"Dans ce livre/roman/film/..."* or *"Dans cette situation..."* The past tense is expressed by the imperfect form of *il s'agissait de...* (It was a question of...; a matter of...)

il arrive	*Il arrive que Georges soit malade.* It happens that Georges is sick.
il reste	*Il nous reste dix francs.* We have 20 francs left.
il vaut [mieux]	*Il vaut mieux lui écrire.* It's better to write him.
il convient	*Il convient de téléphoner.* It's proper to phone.
il suffit de	*Il suffit de m'envoyer une carte postale.* It's enough if you send me a postcard.
il importe de	*Il importe d'arriver à temps.* It's important to arrive on time.

12.3.2 To Make General Observations

Use the formula *il est* + **adjective** + *de* + **infinitive:**

Il est important de bien manger. It's important to eat well.

Est-il nécessaire de le lui dire? Is it necessary to tell it to him?

Il est triste de ne pas la voir. It's sad not to see her.

Il est possible d'être content. It's possible to be happy.

12.3.3 *Il Faut que* + Subjunctive

Il faut que je parte maintenant. I must leave now.

Il ne faut pas que vos amis sachent la vérité. Your friends must not know the truth.

Faut-il que nous venions à midi? Do we have to come at noon?

To **avoid the subjunctive** with *il faut,* use an **indirect object pronoun + the infinitive:**

Il ne lui fallait pas rester. She didn't have to stay.

Est-ce qu'il leur faut déménager? Must they move?

Il nous faudra passer chez eux. We'll have to go by their house.

Vous a-t-il fallu travailler? Did you have to work?

12.4 Idiomatic Expressions with *Être*

être sur le point de faire quelque chose	*Elle est sur le point de se marier.* She's about to get married.
être d'accord	*Es-tu d'accord avec moi?* Do you agree with me?
être en train de	*Nous sommes en train de dîner.* We're in the midst of having dinner.
être plus fort	*C'est plus fort que moi!* I can't help it.
être de l'avis de quelqu'un	*Papa est toujours de ton avis.* Dad always agrees with you.
être de retour	*Le chef sera de retour demain.* The boss will be back tomorrow.
être dans son assiette	*Il n'est pas dans son assiette.* He doesn't feel very well.
être bien	*Êtes-vous bien dans ce lit?* Are you comfortable in that bed?
en être	*Nous en sommes à la page 29.* We're up to page 29.
y être	*J'y suis.* I've got it! (to understand, to "get it")

Problem Solving Example:

Fill in the blanks using the correct idiom forms of expressions using *il* and *être*:

> *Il ne _____ pas beau temps. Il va _____ _____ des nuages et de la pluie. Pierre va aller à la bibliothèque pour choisir des livres d'histoire qui lui plaisent. Jacques n'___ pas _____ _____ _____, il va rester au lit.*

> *Il ne **fait** pas beau temps. Il va **y avoir** des nuages et de la pluie. Pierre va aller à la bibliothèque pour choisir des livres d'histoire qui lui plaisent. Jacques n'**est** pas **dans son assiette**, il va rester au lit.*

12.5 The Verb *Manquer*

Manquer: to miss, to fail, to be short of, "nearly"

***J'ai manqué** le train.* I missed the train.

*Ne **manquez pas** de nous avertir.* Don't fail to let us know.

*As-tu tout l'argent nécessaire? —Non, **il me manque** cinq francs.* Do you have all the money you need? —No, I'm five francs short.

*Elise **a manqué de** tomber.* Elise nearly fell.

Note: "Missing someone" is expressed by "He/she **is missing to me**" rather than by "I miss him/her":

*Pierre est parti; **il nous manque**.* Pierre left; we miss him.

*Où est Agnes? Elle **me manque**.* Where's Agnes? I miss her.

*Puisque leur mère habitait très loin, **elle leur manquait**.* Since their mother lived very far away, they missed her.

*Quand tu seras en vacances sans Anne, **tu lui manqueras**.* When you're on vacation without Anne, she'll miss you.

12.6 Measuring Time with *depuis/depuis que*

To express the passage of time from one point in the past to another point, either in the past alone or including the present, use *depuis* **+ measure of time:**

> *Marc étudie le piano depuis deux ans.* Marc has been studying the piano for two years. [The verb is in the **present** because he's still studying.]

> *François travaillait à Boston depuis six mois quand il a rencontré Monique.* Francis had been working in Boston for six months when he met Monique. [The verbs are in the imperfect and *passé composé* because both actions are in the past and do not extend to the present.]

12.6.1 Using *depuis que* with a Subject and Verb

> *Depuis que tu as rencontré Cécile, tu sors plus souvent.* Since you met Cécile, you go out more often.

> *Nous sommes moins nerveux depuis que nous avons un chien.* We've been less nervous since we have a dog.

> *Il ne nous voit plus jamais depuis qu'il s'est blessé.* He never sees us anymore since he was hurt.

Note: Don't confuse *depuis* (since) with *pendant* (during or while):

> *Il a plu pendant la nuit.* It rained during the night.

> *Nous travaillons pendant l'été.* We work during the summer.

Use *pendant que* with a **subject and verb:**

> *Pendant que Maurice parlait, tout le monde s'endormait.* Everyone fell asleep while Maurice was talking.

> *Pendant que j'y pense, prenez la clé.* While I'm thinking of it, take the key.

12.7 *Connaître* and *Savoir*

While both verbs may be translated as "to know," French differentiates between knowing people, places, works of art (including wine!), i.e., what one learns primarily through the senses, and things that one learns intellectually, by studying, practicing, or learning.

Mon frère connaît bien Rome et Paris mais je connais mieux New York et Los Angeles. My brother knows Rome and Paris well but I know New York and Los Angeles better.

Connaissez-vous les Duval? Savez-vous leur adresse? Do you know the Duvals? Do you know their address?

Jeanne connaît un bon restaurant où l'on sait préparer une bouillabaisse formidable. Jeanne knows a good restaurant where they know how to make a great fish stew.

Savent-ils que ta voiture est en panne? Connaissent-ils un garagiste honnête? Do they know that your car broke down? Are they acquainted with an honest mechanic?

Elle connaît la musique de Chopin et elle sait la jouer aussi. She knows Chopin's music and how to play it, too.

Problem Solving Example:

Fill in the blanks using the correct forms of *manquer*, *depuis/depuis que* or *connaître* and *savoir*:

> Je _____ bien l'Amérique. Je pars demain. J'espère ne pas _____ l'avion. J'aimerais bien voir les Deschamps à New York, _____ - vous les Deschamps ou bien _____ - vous leur numéro de téléphone? Sophie Deschamps travaille à New York _____ un an. J'aimerais bien la voir aussi.

> Je **connais** bien l'Amérique. Je pars demain. J'espère ne pas **manquer** l'avion. J'aimerais bien voir les Deschamps à New York, **connaissez**-vous les Deschamps ou bien **savez**-vous leur numéro de téléphone? Sophie Deschamps travaille à New York **depuis** un an. J'aimerais bien la voir aussi.

12.8 Miscellaneous Expressions

vouloir dire:

Que veut dire "ordinateur?" What does *"ordinateur"* **mean?**

se rendre compte de:

Il se rend compte de sa faute. He **realizes** his mistake.

tout de suite:

Venez tout de suite! Come **at once!**

rendre visite à quelqu'un:

Je rendrai visite à ma tante ce weekend. I'll **visit** my aunt this weekend.

Note: *Voir* or *rendre visite* are used for visiting **a person.** *Visiter* is used for **a place:** *Vas-tu visiter Chicago?*

n'en pouvoir plus:

Le pauvre chaton n'en peut plus. The poor kitten is **exhausted.**

passer un examen:

A-t-elle passé l'examen? Did she **take** the test?

réussir à un examen:

Oui, et elle (y)a réussi. Yes, and she **passed** it.

passer une nuit blanche:

Je suis très fatiguée; j'ai passé une nuit blanche. I'm very tired; I **spent a sleepless night.**

à la fois:

Ils sont à la fois gentils et bêtes. They're both nice and foolish **at the same time.**

en même temps:

Nous sommes arrivés en même temps que Julie. We arrived **at the same time** as Julie.

à son gré:

Le dîner était à notre gré. The dinner was **to our liking.**

CHAPTER 13

Negation

13.1 Positive and Negative Adverbial Expressions

There are always **two** parts to a negative expression: *ne* precedes the verb and another expression follows it *(pas, jamais, aucun,* etc.).

encore: still	*Fabian chante-t-il **encore?*** Does Fabian still sing?
ne . . . plus	*Non, il **ne** chante **plus.*** He no longer sings.
toujours: always	*Irène sort-elle **toujours** avec ces jeunes gens?* Does Irene always go out with those young people?
ne . . . jamais	*Elle **ne** sort **jamais** avec eux.* She never goes out with them.
partout: everywhere	*Va-t-elle **partout** ce soir?* Is she going everywhere tonight?
ne . . . nulle part	*Elle **ne** va **nulle part.*** She's not going anywhere.
déjà: already	*Ont-ils **déjà** déjeuné?* Have they already had lunch?
ne . . . pas encore	*Non, ils **ne** sont **pas encore** descendus.* No, they haven't come down yet.

et: both, and	*Nous avons rencontré et Claude et David. Ont-ils téléphoné?* We met Claude and David. Did they call?
ni . . . ni . . . ne	*Ni Claude ni David n'ont téléphoné.* Neither Claude nor David has phoned.

Note: The verb is **plural** in French for **"neither, nor."**

Problem Solving Example:

Fill in the blanks with the correct form of negation:

> *Il est malade, il _____ mange _____. Avant, il sortait partout, maintenant, il _____ va _____ _____.*

> *Il est malade, il **ne** mange **plus**. Avant, il sortait partout, maintenant, il **ne** va **nulle part**.*

13.1.1 Other Negations

ne . . . pas	*Tu n'as pas d'amis ici.* You have no friends here.
ne . . . guère	*Elle n'a guère répondu.* She hardly answered.
ne . . . que	*Elise n'a que deux chapeaux.* Elise has only two hats.
ne . . . aucun	*Il n'a lu aucun livre cet été.* He hasn't read a single book this summer.

Note: *Aucun* can be used as a **pronoun** as well as an **adjective**. It can be masculine or feminine, but it is always **singular**:

> *A-t-elle reçu mes lettres? —Non, aucune n'est arrivée.* Did she receive my letters? No, not one has arrived.

ne . . . personne	***Personne ne** nous a téléphoné.* No one called us.
ne . . . rien	***Rien n'est** important quand on est malade.* Nothing is important when you're sick.
ne . . . ni . . . ni	*Charles **ne** veut **ni** écouter **ni** discuter l'histoire.* Charles neither wants to listen to the story nor to discuss it.

13.2 *Quelque Chose de/Rien de* + Adjective

To express the general idea of "something" or "nothing" + an adjective, use *quelque chose de* or *rien de:*

*Patricia, as-tu **quelque chose d'intéressant** à nous raconter? Non, je n'ai **rien d'important** à vous dire.* Patricia, do you have something interesting to tell us? No, I've nothing of importance to say to you.

*Est-ce que **quelque chose d'amusant** est arrivé? **Rien d'amusant** n'est arrivé.* Did something amusing happen? Nothing amusing took place.

*Avez-vous acheté **quelque chose de délicieux** au marché? Non, il **n'y avait rien de délicieux** à acheter.* Did you buy something delicious in the market? No, there was nothing delicious to buy.

Note: The adjective is always masculine singular in these structures.

For "someone," "anyone," or "nobody" use *quelqu'un de* or *personne de*:

*Connaissent-ils **quelqu'un de** riche et **de** célèbre? Non, ils ne connaissent **personne de** riche ni **de** célèbre.* Do they know anyone rich and famous? No, they don't know anybody who's rich and famous.

*Est-ce que **quelqu'un d'**intelligent ferait cela? Non, **personne d'**intelligent ne le ferait.* Would someone intelligent do that? No, nobody intelligent would do it.

Problem Solving Example:

Q Use *ne . . . personne* and *ne . . . rien* in the following sentences:

As-tu parlé à ta grand-mère aujourd'hui? Moi, je n'ai parlé à _____ parce que je lisais beaucoup. À part cela, je n'ai _____ fait.

*As-tu parlé à ta grand-mère aujourd'hui? Moi, je n'ai parlé à **personne** parce que je lisais beaucoup. À part cela, je n'ai **rien** fait.*

In these examples, "*ne . . . rien*" operates like other negative expressions, where the "*ne*" particle precedes the conjugated verb and "*rien*" follows it. "*Ne . . . personne*" works slightly differently, as "*personne*" replaces a person's name.

Quiz: Idiomatic Expressions and Negation

1. J'ai fini mes études. Je _____ .

    (A) ne vais pas étudier   (C) n'ai pas étudié

    (B) n'étudie plus   (D) n'étudie déjà

2. J'ai échoué à l'examen. Je n'ai pas _____ à l'examen.

    (A) réussi   (C) reçu

    (B) passé   (D) étudié

3. L'hiver était terrible avec la neige abondante, et les petits oiseaux n'avaient _____ .

    (A) plus rien à chanter   (C) plus qu'à manger

    (B) personne à regarder   (D) rien à manger

4. Il n'aime pas le petit dejeuner. Ce n'est pas _____ .

    (A) à son gré   (C) mauvais

    (B) tout de suite   (D) pire

5. Elles sont _____ pauvres et heureuses.

    (A) à même temps   (C) au temps

    (B) à les mêmes temps   (D) à la fois

6. Il ne peut pas aller avec nous ce soir. Il ne va _____.

    (A) nulle part   (B) toujours

    (C) partout   (C) déjà

7. Je _____ veux ni aller au cinéma, _____ rester chez moi.

    (A) ni, ni   (C) ne, ni

    (B) ni, ne   (D) ne, ne

8. L'ordinateur est en panne. _____ peut utiliser l'ordinateur.

    (A) Rien ne   (C) Personne ne

    (B) Pas ne   (D) Tout le monde

9. Elle adore les grandes villes, alors elle _____ New York souvent.

    (A) ne rend pas visite   (C) rend visite

    (B) ne visite pas   (D) visite

10. <u>Pas un</u> étudiant <u>n</u>' a répondu à ma question.

    (A) Aucuns . . . n'   (C) Nulle . . . __

    (B) Nul . . . __   (D) Aucun . . . n'

ANSWER KEY

1.	(B)	6.	(A)
2.	(A)	7.	(C)
3.	(D)	8.	(C)
4.	(A)	9.	(D)
5.	(D)	10.	(D)

CHAPTER 14

Useful Vocabulary

14.1 School (l'École)

l'assistance (f.) – attendance   *le collège* – middle school

assister au cours – to attend class   *un mémoire* – a paper

la manifestation – demonstration   *échouer, rater* – to fail

obtenir son diplôme – to graduate   *la lecture* – reading

l'horaire (m.) – class schedule   *réussir* – to pass

la biblio(thèque) – the library   *la librairie* – the bookstore

l'ordinateur (m.) – computer   *la conférence* – lecture

sa spécialisation – one's major   *le lycée* – high school

s'inscrire aux cours – to register for classes

l'école élémentaire (f.) – grammar school

des livres d'occasion (m.) – used books

des cours obligatoires (m.) – required classes

14.2 Animals (un Animal; les Animaux)

le bœuf – bull   *la vache* – cow

le cerf – deer   *la biche* – doe

le coq – rooster   *la poule* – hen

le mouton – sheep   *le chat* – tomcat

le chien – dog   *un cheval* – horse

un mulet(m.)/ *une mule*(f.) – mule   *un lapin* – rabbit

un âne – donkey   *un renard* – fox

un poisson – a fish   *un oiseau* – bird

un ours – bear

14.3 The Body *(le Corps)*

la tête – head
la joue – cheek
les oreilles (f.) – ears
la chevelure – head of hair
les lèvres (f.) – lips
la langue – tongue
la poitrine – chest
la jambe – leg
le pied – foot
le bras – arm
le poignet – wrist
le dos – the back
le cœur – heart

un œil; les yeux – one eye, the
    eyes
les cheveux (m.) – hair
la bouche – mouth
les dents (f.) – teeth
le cou – neck
le ventre – stomach
le genou – knee
la cheville – ankle
le coude – elbow
la main – hand
l'épaule (f.) – shoulder
le foie – liver

14.4 The City *(la Ville)*

le centre ville – downtown
visiter la ville – sightseeing in
    town
une visite – a tour
Où se trouve...? – Where is...?
à gauche – to the left
à droite – to the right
tout droit – straight ahead
la place – the square
la rue – the street
le boulevard – the boulevard
le musée – the museum
le parc – the park
la préfecture – police station
le bureau de poste – post office
Renseignements (m.) –
    Information (booth)
le jardin zoologique – the zoo

la cité – the old part of town
une excursion – a guided sight-
    seeing tour
l'hôtel de ville (m.)– town hall
la fontaine – fountain
le trottoir – the sidewalk
le cinéma – the movies
le tarif, droit d'entrée – admission fee
un banc – a bench
les chèques de voyage (m.) –
    traveler's checks
l'immeuble (m.) – building
la banque – the bank
l'agent de police (m.) – policeman
des timbres (m.) – stamps
l'agence de voyage (f.)– travel
    agency

14.5 Clothing *(les Vêtements)*

un chemisier – a blouse	*une jupe* – a skirt
un pantalon – pants	*un chapeau* – a hat
un sac – a purse	*une robe* – a dress
les chaussures (f.) – shoes	*un tailleur* – a lady's suit
un maillot de bain – a bathing suit	*les gants* (m.) – gloves
la veste – a jacket (suit)	*un blouson* – outside jacket
un manteau – a coat	*une écharpe* (f.) – scarf
des bas (m.) – stockings	*le short* – shorts
un peignoir – a bathrobe	*le bleu-jean* – jeans
l'imperméable (l'imper) (m.) – a raincoat	*le tricot, le pull, le chandail* – sweater, pullover
les chaussettes (f.) – socks	*une ceinture* – belt
un complet – a man's suit	*une chemise* – a shirt
une cravate – a tie	*un gilet* – a vest
le linge – linen	*la manche* – sleeve

Problem Solving Example:

Choose the correct word and/or correct spelling in parentheses:

> *La petite fille va à (l'école, l'ordinateur). Elle aime lire à (la bibliothèque, des livres d'occasion). Elle aime marcher au (parc, banque) et porter (une cravate, une robe).*

> *La petite fille va à l'école. Elle aime lire à la bibliothèque. Elle aime marcher au parc et porter une robe.*

L'école is correct because the preposition *à* is used. Remember that "to the" is expressed by either *à la* (for feminine words) or *au* (for masculine words). Because *à* is used instead of *au*, *l'école* is the correct answer. The same explanation applies to *la bibliothèque*, which is the next correct answer. *Parc* must be correct because it is masculine and only masculine words can follow *au*. (Remember also that *au* is the contraction of *à + le*). *Une robe* is correct because it means "a dress,"

whereas *une cravate* means "a man's tie"—hardly a logical choice for a little girl to wear.

14.6 Colors *(les Couleurs)*

le bleu – blue   *le pourpre* – purple   *le rouge* – red
le gris – gray   *le beige* – beige   *le vert* – green
le noir – black   *le jaune* – yellow   *le brun* – brown
le rose – pink   *le blanc* – white   *le marron* – chestnut brown

14.7 Drinks *(les Boissons)*

le vin – wine
la bière – beer
l'eau minérale (f.) – mineral water
la citronnade – lemonade
le coca – Coke
une boisson gazeuse – a soft drink
le café crème – coffee with cream
le café noir – black coffee
le café express – espresso coffee
le café décaféiné – decaffeinated coffee
le thé – tea
le thé glacé – iced tea
le chocolat chaud – hot chocolate

un demi – glass of beer
le jus de fruits – fruit juice
la limonade – soda (7-Up)
le soda – club soda
le café – coffee
le café au lait – coffee with milk
le café turc – Turkish coffee
le lait – milk
un café serré – small cup of coffee, black, very strong
le thé anglais – tea with milk
un apéritif (l'apéro) – cocktail
un digestif – a liqueur; after-dinner drink

14.8 The Family *(la Famille)*

le père – the father
un bébé – a baby
un garçon – a boy
le fils – the son
la tante – the aunt
la grand-mère – the grandmother
le cousin, la cousine – the cousin
la nièce – the niece

la mère – the mother
un(e) enfant – a child (boy or girl)
une fille – a girl, a daughter
papa, maman – dad, mom
l'oncle – the uncle
le grand-père – the grandfather
le neveu – the nephew

14.9 Foods *(les Aliments)*

Fruits *(les Fruits):*

une banane – banana
une poire – pear
une prune – plum
une cerise – cherry
une fraise – strawberry
un ananas – pineapple
un pamplemousse – grapefruit

une pomme – apple
une pêche – peach
une orange – orange
un abricot – apricot
une framboise – raspberry
un citron – lemon
les raisins secs (m.) – raisins

Vegetables *(les Légumes):*

une carotte – carrot
une pomme de terre – potato
un oignon – onion
le maïs – corn
les brocolis (m.) – broccoli
le poivron – pepper
    (red or green)

une tomate – tomato
la laitue – lettuce
les haricots (m.) – beans
les petits pois (m.) – peas
les épinards (m.) – spinach
le concombre – cucumber

Meat and Poultry *(la Viande et la Volaille):*

le bœuf – beef
le veau – veal
le porc – pork
le mouton – lamb
le canard – duck

le bifteck – steak
le jambon – ham
les saucisses (f.) – sausage
le poulet – chicken
la dinde – turkey

Desserts *(les Desserts):*

la tarte aux pommes – apple pie
la glace – ice cream
la crème brûlée – custard
un beignet – a doughnut
une crêpe – a thin pancake
la pâtisserie – pastry
le gâteau au chocolat –
    chocolate cake

la tarte aux fruits – fruit pie
les parfums (m.) – the flavors
un petit gâteau – cookie
le gaufre – waffle
le yaourt – yogurt
un chou à la crème – a cream puff

Problem Solving Example:

Q Correct the spelling in the passage below:

> *Marie mange beaucoup de fraise et d'abricot. Elle a des beau œils et des dants très blanq. Elle va au lycé et elle voudrait un jour aller à l'université. Elle porte toujours un jupe ou une robe avec un seinture.*

> *Marie mange beaucoup de fraise(s) et d'abricot(s). Elle a de beau(x) **yeux** et des **dents** très **blanches**. Elle va au lycé(e) et elle voudrait un jour aller à l'université. Elle porte toujours un(e) jupe ou une robe avec un(e) **ceinture**.*

Fraises and *abricots* are both plural, meaning "strawberries" and "apricots." The plural form of *beau* is *beaux* describing *yeux* (eyes) the plural form. *Dents* is the correct spelling for teeth. *Blanches* is plural feminine describing teeth. *Lycée* is the correct spelling for "high school." *Une* is the correct indefinite article since *jupe* (skirt) is feminine. *Une* is the correct indefinite article since *ceinture*, the correct spelling of the word meaning "belt", is feminine.

14.10   Illnesses *(les Maladies)*

avoir mal . . . – to have pain . . .

aller chez le médecin – to go to the doctor's office

avoir des frissons – to have chills

la tension – blood pressure

avoir des nausées – to be nauseous

l'antibiotique (m.) – antibiotic

la piqûre – an injection

une démangeaison – an itching

un rhume – a cold

l'hôpital (m.) – hospital

l'ordonnance (f.) – prescription

être allergique à – to be allergic (to)

la douleur – pain

le pouls – pulse

vomir – to vomit

le médicament – medicine

une pilule – a pill

une éruption – a rash

la grippe – the flu

l'infirmière (f.) – the nurse

les honoraires (m.) – doctor's fee

14.11 Professions, Occupations (*les Professions, les Métiers*)

Note: For many professions, there is no female form. The words *femme* or *une* precede the profession or the masculine form is used.

un(e) avocat(e) – lawyer

un ingénieur – engineer

un, une secrétaire – secretary

une actrice – actress

un chauffeur de taxi – taxi driver

un serveur, une serveuse – waiter, waitress

un commis – clerk

la ménagère – housewife

le fermier, la fermière – farmer

un pilote – pilot

un musicien, une musicienne – musician

le pharmacien, la pharmacienne – pharmacist

un juge – judge

un chef – cook or department head

un acteur – actor

un, une artiste – artist

un professeur – secondary or college teacher

un vendeur, une vendeuse – salesperson

le coiffeur, la coiffeuse – hairdresser

le policier, la policière – policeman, policewoman

le banquier – banker

un chimiste – chemist

Quiz: Useful Vocabulary

1. Il y avait beaucoup de monde à la _____ sur l'oeuvre de Balzac.

    (A) conférence   (C) manifestation

    (B) lecture   (D) porte-parole

2. À la pâtisserie, on achète _____.

    (A) des saucisses   (C) des gâteaux

    (B) des raisins secs   (D) des parfums

3. Cet _____ est très connu.

    (A) restaurant   (C) jardin

    (B) maison   (D) hôtel

4. Il s'est lavé _____.

    (A) ses cheveux   (C) sa figure

    (B) la figure   (D) ses mains

5. J'adore les légumes! Donnez-moi _____.

    (A) une carotte

    (B) une tarte aux pommes

    (C) du mouton

    (D) une gaufre

6. Elle était sur le sable, la peau toute brûlée par _____.

    (A) la mer   (C) le soleil

    (B) le ciel   (D) le sable

7. Quand on s'habille, on met _____ dans les manches des vêtements.

    (A) les pieds   (C) les genoux

    (B) les bras   (D) les jambes

8. Tout ce linge sale! Bon, alors samedi je ferai . . .

    (A) la lessive   (C) une plainte

    (B) la grasse matinée   (D) la vaisselle

9. Quelle bonne . . . ! Tu as les joues toutes roses!

    (A) fleur   (C) mine

    (B) jardinière   (D) recette

10. C'est la deuxième . . . que tu as fait cette faute!

    (A) temps   (C) heure

    (B) fois   (D) époque

ANSWER KEY

1.	(A)		6.	(C)
2.	(C)		7.	(B)
3.	(D)		8.	(A)
4.	(B)		9.	(C)
5.	(A)		10.	(B)

CHAPTER 15

Reading Passages

Throughout this book you have acquired the skills needed to speak and understand French. You have been tested on individual points of grammar, usage, and vocabulary. All of the elements are combined in the reading passages that follow. Read through them and use the questions after each passage to test your comprehension.

Reading Passage #1

Cassis, le 2 juillet 1999

Cher Arnaud,

Vendredi soir, Stéphane, Adèle, Gabrielle, et moi, nous sommes allés au cinéma. Comme d'habitude, Stéphane n'est pas arrivé à l'heure. Il est arrivé en retard parce qu'il avait des problèmes avec sa voiture. Nous sommes partis de chez moi vers vingt heures et demie. Malheureusement, nous sommes arrivés au cinéma après le début du film. Mais comme il y avait des problèmes techniques, ils ont recommencé le film dès le début. Donc, nous n'avons rien raté! Quelle chance! On a vu *les Nuits fauves*. C'était génial! Après le film, nous sommes allés au café où on a pris des cocas.

Nous avons longtemps parlé de nos vacances d'été, et je suis vraiment contente d'avoir rencontré Stéphane et Adèle, et surtout Gaby. Elle va me manquer à la rentrée. Gaby m'a emmenée chez moi vers minuit. Et j'ai bien dormi ce soir-là parce que j'avais fait tant de belles choses!

Samedi, je suis allée à la plage avec mon frère. On s'est bien amusés! Après, nous sommes allés au marché avec Maman, et puis on a préparé un dîner en famille. Qu'est-ce qu'on a bien mangé! Ma tante Danielle et mon oncle Claude ont amené mes cousins, et on a joué au Scrabble après le dessert.

Tu me manques et j'espère que tout va bien avec toi et ta famille.

Ciao!

Mimi

Problem Solving Example:

1. *Combien de personnes sont allés au cinéma?*
2. *Qui est toujours en retard?*
3. *Est-ce qu'ils ont vu tout le film?*
4. *Quelle était la réaction au film?*
5. *Qu'est-ce que Mimi et ses amis ont commandé au café?*
6. *Quel ami est très cher à Mimi?*
7. *Qu'est-ce que Mimi a fait le lendemain?*
8. *Selon la lettre, qui était au dîner samedi soir?*

1. *Quatre personnes sont allés au cinéma. (Mimi, Stéphane, Adèle, et Gabrielle)*
2. *Stéphane est toujours en retard.*
3. *Ils ont raté le film, mais à cause des problèmes techniques, le projectionniste a recommencé le film.*
4. *Mimi et ses amis ont aimé le film, "c'était génial!"*
5. *Ils ont commandé des cocas.*
6. *Gaby (Gabrielle) est très chère à Mimi.*
7. *Mimi est allée à la plage avec son frère, elle est allée au marché avec sa mère, elle a préparé un dîner en famille, puis elle a joué au Scrabble.*
8. *Mimi, sa mère, son frère, sa tante Danielle, son oncle Claude, et leurs enfants.*

Reading Passage #2

Les empereurs romains étaient tous de grands bâtisseurs, et la plupart de leurs constructions avaient pour but l'utilité publique et la satisfaction des besoins de la personne moyenne. Parmi leurs monuments sont des théâtres, des cirques, des temples, des basiliques ou palais de justice, des thermes ou établissements de bains, des aqueducs, des arcs de triomphe, et des portiques.

Rome s'est couvert de monuments grandioses, de proportions souvent colossales, qui ont embelli la ville et ont donné du travail aux ouvriers. Auguste a ajouté un nouveau forum à l'ancien, a fait bâtir le théâtre de Marcellus et le Panthéon, temple destiné à abriter tous les dieux de l'univers. Après l'incendie de Rome, Néron a relevé sur un plan régulier les quartiers détruits et s'est fait construire un palais si luxueux que l'on l'a appelé la Maison Dorée.

Problem Solving Example:

1. *Pourquoi est-ce que les empereurs romains ont construit de grands bâtiments?*
2. *Quels sont trois types de monuments romans?*
3. *Comment est-ce qu'on caractérise les monuments romains?*
4. *Qui a réintroduit un type d'architecture à l'ancien?*
5. *Quel empereur a renouvelé Rome après des événements catastrophiques?*

1. *Les Empereurs romains ont construit de grands bâtiments pour l'utilité publique, pour la satisfaction du peuple, et pour créer des monuments afin de marquer leurs règnes.*
2. *Les types de monuments sont des théâtres, des cirques, et des temples (on peut dire aussi des basiliques ou palais de justice, des thermes ou établissements de bains, des aqueducs, des arcs de triomphe, et des portiques).*
3. *Les monuments romains sont grandioses.*
4. *Auguste a réintroduit un nouveau forum à l'ancien.*
5. *Néron a renouvelé Rome après des incendies.*

Reading Passage #3

Le Tartuffe est l'une des grandes pièces de Molière; elle a été jouée en 1664 pour la première fois. Dans la maison d'Orgon, "la vie est trop mondaine," proclame Tartuffe, directeur de conscience invité. C'est par son austérité qu'il a séduit le maître, et il n'est pas convenable qu'il y ait tant de rires, tant de projets frivoles. Masqué derrière la rigueur de son discours proliférant, il devient progressivement parasite des biens matériels, des hommes, des relations, et il jouit en cachette de tous les plaisirs qu'il vole et qu'il interdit aux autres. Perfide, transgressant la foi, il détruit autour de lui les systèmes de confiance et initie ainsi un processus de désagrégation de la société. Même avec une fin heureuse quasi-miraculeuse, personne ne peut sortir indemne d'une telle contagion.

Problem Solving Example:

1. *Qui a écrit la pièce Le Tartuffe?*
2. *À votre avis, est-ce que Tartuffe possède beaucoup de pouvoir?*
3. *Au début de la pièce, comment est la maison d'Orgon?*
4. *Selon ce passage existe-t-il des changements notables dans ce petit monde à la fin de la pièce?*

1. *Molière a écrit Le Tartuffe.*
2. *Oui, Tartuffe possède beaucoup de pouvoir. Il séduit Orgon et il commence à réussir à ses projets. Notamment, il trompe les gens en interdisant ses propres plaisirs aux autres.*
3. *Chez Orgon, 'la vie est trop mondaine," c'est-à-dire, superficielle.*
4. *Oui, Tartuffe a renversé l'ordre de la famille d'Orgon. Même si la fin est heureuse, "personne ne peut sortir indemne d'une telle contagion;" tout le monde est marqué.*

Reading Passage #4

Claude Monet est né en 1840. Originaire de Paris, il passait sa jeunesse au Havre. Il a commencé sa carrière comme caricaturiste. À l'âge de dix-sept ans, ses œuvres étaient présentées dans la vitrine d'un encadreur où l'on pouvait voir les tableaux d'autres artistes.

Quand Claude avait dix-neuf ans, il est parti pour étudier la peinture à Paris. Il s'est inscrit à l'Académie suisse, où il a fait la connaissance d'un autre peintre célebre, Pissarro. Sous l'enseignement du maître Charles Gleyre, Monet a formé un groupe d'amis-artistes, composé de Bazille, Renoir, et Sisley. Pendant sa vie, Monet collaborait avec d'autres artistes connus, comme Edouard Manet.

La gloire de Monet vient principalement de sa peinture la plus connue, *Impression, soleil levant,* qui a donné, lors d'une exposition des Indépendants, le nom du groupe Impressioniste. Cherchant sans cesse, il allait toujours plus loin pour traduire l'impression première, le moment fugitif où le regard rencontre le paysage.

À partir de 1883, Monet s'est installé à Giverny. Son jardin, le pont japonais, le bassin aux Nymphéas font partie de son œuvre, de la même façon que ses tableaux. Cette propriété existe toujours et fait partie d'une fondation qui sert comme musée pendant les mois d'avril au octobre. Malheureusement, Monet est mort aveugle à l'âge de 86 ans.

Problem Solving Example:

1. *Est-ce que Monet a commencé sa carrière comme peintre?*
2. *Quand est-ce que Monet a fait son début dans le monde professionnel de la peinture?*
3. *Travaillait-il seul?*
4. *D'où vient le mot "Impressioniste"?*
5. *Quel est l'état actuel de la maison de Monet à Giverny?*
6. *Nommez trois lieux importants à Giverny.*

1. *Non, il a commencé sa carrière comme caricaturiste.*
2. *Monet a fait son début dans le monde professionnel de la peinture à l'âge de 17 ans.*

3. *Non, Monet travaillait avec ses amis Bazille, Renoir, Sisley, et Edouard Manet.*
4. *Le mot "Impressioniste" vient du tableau* **Impression, soleil levant.**
5. *Sa maison à Giverny est maintenant un musée.*
6. *La maison à Giverny se compose du jardin, du pont japonais, et du bassin aux Nymphéas.*

Reading Passage #5

Le kathak est une danse classique du Nord de l'Inde, dont Delhi est le principal foyer. Enseigné autrefois aux prostituées et courtisanes par des maîtres de danse, il est installé aujourd'hui dans l'académie. Généralement exécutée en solo, cette danse est souvent accompagnée de mimes racontant des épisodes du *Mahabharta* ou du *Ramayana*, les deux grands textes mythologiques de l'Inde.

Un guru célèbre, Biriju Maharaj, est issu d'une dynastie légendaire de maîtres de danse kathak, dont il représente la septième génération d'artistes. Danseur inégale et remarquable pédagogue, il chante, compose de la musique de danse, joue une multitude d'instruments de percussion, et écrit des poèmes. Biriju Maharaj amplifie la forme classique du kathak en y introduisant des compositions de groupe basées sur des thèmes mythologiques, historiques et contemporains.

Problem Solving Example:

1. *Est-ce que le kathak est une danse qui se fait partout en Asie?*
2. *Peut-on dire que l'image du kathak a changé depuis ses origines?*
3. *Qui est Biriju Maharaj?*
4. *Quels sont les talents de Biriju Maharaj?*
5. *Le kathak, c'est une danse traditionnelle?*

1. *Non, c'est une danse d'origine indienne.*
2. *Oui, au début, le kathak était une danse des prostituées et des courtisanes; maintenant, c'est une danse qui est entrée dans l'académie.*
3. *Biriju Maharaj est connu comme un guru célèbre du kathak, d'une famille de danseurs de kathak.*
4. *Il enseigne la danse, il chante, il compose de la musique, il joue des instruments, il écrit des poèmes, etc.*
5. *Oui, le kathak est une danse traditionnelle, à cause de ses éléments mythologiques et historiques.*

Reading Passage #6

Jason était le héros de Thessalie. Héros navigateur, il s'est emparé de la Toison d'or, une dépouille précieuse d'un bélier divin que gardait un dragon sur les terres du roi de Colchide, au pied du Caucase. Pour aller la conquérir, Jason a construit le navire Argo, que montaient cinquante héros, appelés les Argonautes. La toison a été enlevée grâce aux enchantements de la magicienne Médée, fille du roi de Colchide. Médée a suivi Jason dans son voyage merveilleux. Mais abandonnée par lui pour une autre femme, elle a égorgé ses enfants et sa rivale, puis elle s'est enfuie en Attique où elle est devenue l'épouse d'Egée, roi d'Athènes, père de Thésée.

Problem Solving Example:

1. *Qu'est-ce que c'est que la Toison d'or?*
2. *Où se trouve Colchide?*
3. *Qui est le roi de Colchide?*
4. *Qu'est-ce que c'est que l'Argo?*
5. *Qui a aidé Jason à prendre la toison?*
6. *Est-ce que Médée a protégé son pays?*
7. *Médée est-elle restée chez elle après la guerre?*
8. *Est-ce que Jason et Médée ont fini leurs jours ensemble?*
9. *Médée est-elle méchante?*
10. *A la fin de l'histoire, où habitait Médée?*

1. *La Toison d'or est la dépouille précieuse d'un bélier divin que gardait un dragon sur les terres du roi de Colchide.*
2. *Colchide se trouve au pied du Caucase (des montagnes).*
3. *Le roi de Colchide est le père de Médée.*
4. *L'Argo est le navire (une espèce de bateau), construit par Jason pour contenir cinquante héros (les Argonautes).*
5. *Grâce à ses enchantements magiques, Médée a aidé à prendre la Toison d'or.*
6. *Non, Médée a trahi son pays: elle a libéré le dragon quand elle a volé la Toison d'or, puis elle est partie avec l'ennemi de son pays, Jason.*
7. *Non, elle est partie avec Jason.*
8. *Non, elle a tué ses enfants et la femme de Jason, puis elle s'est enfuie en Attique pour devenir la femme du roi d'Athènes.*
9. *Oui, elle est méchante; Médée a tué ses enfants et la femme de Jason pour démontrer sa haine pour lui.*
10. *Elle habitait avec Egée, le roi d'Athènes.*

Reading Passage #7

Charles Baudelaire est connu partout dans le monde comme le poète français le plus important. Il est né à Paris le 9 avril 1821. Malgré les espoirs de suivre une carrière diplomatique qu'avaient pour lui sa mère et son beau-père, Charles ne voulait être qu'écrivain. À Paris, il fréquentait la jeunesse littéraire du Quartier Latin, où il faisait la connaissance d'autres poètes et artistes. Étant l'ami de Théophile Gautier, de Gérard de Nerval, de Sainte-Beuve, et de Théodore de Banville, Baudelaire participait à l'un des mouvements affectés, le dandysme. Cette vie excentrique lui causait beaucoup de dettes. Après avoir été soumis à un conseil judiciaire (provoqué par sa mère et son beau-père, le général Aupick) Baudelaire se sentait humilié.

Pendant cette période d'humiliation, Baudelaire continuait à travailler des poèmes, en écrivant des articles de critique pour gagner sa vie. En 1846, Baudelaire a découvert l'œuvre d'Edgar Poe, l'écrivain américain, qui était incompris et maudit, lui aussi. À cause de leur ressemblance, Baudelaire a décidé de traduire les écrits de son semblable, un projet qui occupait dix-sept années de sa vie. La publication des *Fleurs de mal* en 1857 a valu à Baudelaire le renom dont il jouit aujourd'hui. Le gouvernement a trouvé ce livre obscène et scandaleux. Par conséquent, Baudelaire a payé une forte amende, et plusieurs poèmes ont été supprimés.

Pendant les dix dernières années de sa vie, Baudelaire souffrait des crises gastriques. Après un séjour en Belgique en 1866, il a subi une attaque de paralysie qui l'a rendu presque muet. Pendant un an, il agonisait, et il est mort à l'âge de 46 ans le 31 août 1867.

L'influence de Baudelaire a été capitale, tant en France qu'à l'étranger. Obsédé par le mal, Baudelaire savait faire de la douleur une noblesse. Passionné de tout art, la musique, la peinture, et la poésie, il savait aussi donner à sa poésie une mélodie et une résonance profondes. Il est connu comme le premier poète "moderne", et toute la poésie française est marquée par le génie de ce poète maudit.

Problem Solving Example:

1. *Charles a-t-il suivi les conseils de sa famille?*
2. *Où est-ce que Charles a passé son temps à Paris?*
3. *Quel mouvement a inspiré Baudelaire?*
4. *Après avoir contracté des dettes, qu'est-ce qui est arrivé à Charles?*
5. *Quel écrivain étranger a inspiré Baudelaire? Pourquoi?*
6. *Est-ce que la publication des Fleurs du mal était un succès pour Baudelaire?*
7. *Baudelaire a-t-il fini sa vie en paix?*
8. *Aimait-il d'autres formes artistiques?*
9. *Est-ce que Baudelaire influence beaucoup de gens?*

1. *Non, Charles n'a pas suivi la carrière diplomatique suggérée par sa mère et son beau-père.*
2. *Charles passait son temps à Paris dans le Quartier Latin.*
3. *Le dandysme a inspiré l'art de Baudelaire.*
4. *Après avoir contracté des dettes, Baudelaire a été soumis à un conseil judiciaire.*

5. *Le poète américain Edgar Poe a inspiré Baudelaire parce qu'il était considéré comme un poète maudit.*

6. *La publication des Fleurs du mal a jetté Baudelaire dans la lumière du succès, mais il a été soumis à un procès, il a payé une forte amende, et il a dû supprimer plusieurs poèmes dans les éditions successives.*

7. *Non, il souffrait des douleurs.*

8. *Oui, il aimait la musique et la peinture.*

9. *Oui, il influence des gens partout dans le monde.*

CHAPTER 16

Glossary

aïeul; aïeux (m.) – ancestor; ancestors
aile (f.) – wing
à la carte – from the menu (singly chosen items)
Allemagne (f.) – Germany
allemand(e) (adj.) – German
américain(e) (adj.) – American
Américain(e) – American person
animé(e) (adj.) – lively; busy
au pair (m.) – a person who works for room and board

berger (m.) – shepherd
beurre (m.) – butter
bœuf (m.) – beef; ox; steer
boire – to drink
boisson (f.) – a drink
bonheur (m.) – happiness
bonté (f.) – kindness
bout (m.) – end; bottom
breton(ne) (adj.) – Breton (from Brittany)
bureau (m.) – desk; office

cadet (m.) – younger of two children; youngest
caisse (f.) – cash register (where you pay a bill)
campagne (f.) – countryside
chaîne (f.) – TV channel
chef-d'oeuvre (m.) – masterpiece
chèque (m.) – check (bank)

chez – at the house of
chiffon (m.) – rag
choisir – to choose
chronique (f.) – chronicle; newspaper column
clé; clef (f.) – key
coiffeuse (f.) – hairdresser; dressing table
commencer – to begin
compter – to count
concours (m.) – contest
connaître – to know; be acquainted with
conseiller – to advise
cou (m.) – neck
coup d'état (m.) – sudden overthrow of a government
coup de grâce (m.) – death blow
craindre – to fear
croire – to believe

debout (adv., adj.; invariable) – standing
déception (f.) – disappointment
déçu (adj.) – disappointed
de luxe (adj.) – luxurious
demain (m.) – tomorrow
demander – to ask
détente (f.) – easing of political tensions, recreation
dette (f.) – debt
deuil (m.) – mourning
devoir– 1. to have to do something; 2. *(noun; m.)* duty
dire – to say; tell

eau (f.) – water
écrire – to write
empêcher – to prevent; impede
emporter – to carry off; take something along
enfant (m., f.) – child
enseigner – to teach
entendre – to hear; understand
envoyer – to send

essayer – to try
éteindre – to extinguish; shut off
étendre – to stretch

faire – to make; to do
fait accompli (m.) – accomplished fact; a "done deed"
faveur (f.) – favor
fête (f.) – party; festival; feast

fontaine (f.) – fountain
force de frappe (f.) – striking force (army)
français (adj., m.) – French (language or thing)
Français(e) (m., f.) – Frenchman; Frenchwoman

garçon (m.) – boy; waiter
gare (f.) – railway station
gêne (f.) – embarrassment; discomfort; trouble
gilet (m.) – vest; cardigan
gourmand (adj., m.) – a big eater
gourmet (m.) – a discriminating eater
grand prix (m.) – first prize
guêpe (f.) – wasp
guérir – to cure; heal
guerre (f.) – war

habiter – to live (in a place); reside
haïr – to hate
haut; haute (adj.) – high; loud
hier (m.) – yesterday

imiter – to imitate
inégal(e) – unequal
irréel (f.) – unreal

jaune (adj.) – yellow
jeune (adj.) – young

klaxon (m.) – car horn
liaison (f.) – a relationship; linking of consonant and vowel
lisse (adj.) – smooth; sleek

mal – 1. *(noun, m.)* evil; pain;
     2. *(adverb)* badly
mèche (f.) – lock of hair; wick
médecin (m.) – doctor
médecine (f.) – the profession of medicine
médicament (m.) – medication
même (adj) – 1. same; 2. self; 3. very same
menace (f.) – a threat
mener – to lead someone
merveille (f.) – marvel
mois (m.) – month
mot-clé (m.) – key word
moulin (m.) – mill

naissance (f.) – birth
naître – to be born
négation (f.) – negative forms; negation
neige (f.) – snow
nom (m.) – name; noun
nuage (m.) – cloud

œil; yeux (m.) – eye; eyes
œuf (m.) – egg
ôter – 1. to remove; 2. lift; 3. take away
ou – or
où –where
ouest (m.) – west
ouïr – to hear

paix (f.) – peace
palais (m.) – 1. palace; 2. palate
pareil; pareille – similar; the same
peine (f.) – 1. sorrow, sadness; 2. effort
plaisir (m.) – pleasure
profond (adj.) – deep; profound

quai (m.) – dock; wharf

raconter – to recount; tell a story
rencontrer – to meet; encounter someone

rester – to stay; remain
rhume (m.) – a cold
rire – to laugh

sale (adj.) – dirty
salle (f.) – room
sauce (f.) – gravy; salad dressing; sauce
savoir – to know
sec (adj.) – dry
sécheresse (f.) – drought
sel (m.) – salt

soif (f.) – thirst
soir (m.) – evening
sortie (f.) – 1. exit; 2. military action
souffrir – to suffer
soulier (m.) – shoe

tête (f.) – head
tirade (f.) – long speech in a play; tirade
tôt (adj.) – early
travail (m.) – work
travailler – to work
trompe-l'œil (m.) – style of art that appears to be something it isn't
trou (m.) – hole
trouver – to find

usine (f.) – factory
utile – useful

vérité (f.) – truth
vif (adj.) – lively; bright (color)
vilain (adj.) – ugly; nasty; wicked
visiter – to see (a place, not a person); to tour
voir – to see

wagon (m.) – railway car

REA's **Test Preps**
The Best in Test Preparation

- REA "Test Preps" are **far more** comprehensive than any other test preparation series
- Each book contains up to **eight** full-length practice tests based on the most recent exams
- **Every** type of question likely to be given on the exams is included
- Answers are accompanied by **full** and **detailed** explanations

REA publishes over 60 Test Preparation volumes in several series. They include:

Advanced Placement Exams (APs)
Biology
Calculus AB & Calculus BC
Chemistry
Economics
English Language & Composition
English Literature & Composition
European History
Government & Politics
Physics B & C
Psychology
Spanish Language
Statistics
United States History

College-Level Examination Program (CLEP)
Analyzing and Interpreting Literature
College Algebra
Freshman College Composition
General Examinations
General Examinations Review
History of the United States I
History of the United States II
Human Growth and Development
Introductory Sociology
Principles of Marketing
Spanish

SAT Subject Tests
Biology E/M
Chemistry
English Language Proficiency Test
French
German

SAT Subject Tests (cont'd)
Literature
Mathematics Level 1, 2
Physics
Spanish
United States History
Writing

Graduate Record Exams (GREs)
Biology
Chemistry
Computer Science
General
Literature in English
Mathematics
Physics
Psychology

ACT - ACT Assessment

ASVAB - Armed Services Vocational Aptitude Battery

CBEST - California Basic Educational Skills Test

CDL - Commercial Driver License Exam

CLAST - College Level Academic Skills Test

COOP & HSPT - Catholic High School Admission Tests

ELM - California State University Entry Level Mathematics Exam

FE (EIT) - Fundamentals of Engineering Exams - For both AM & PM Exams

FTCE - Florida Teacher Certification Exam

GED - High School Equivalency Diploma Exam (U.S. & Canadian editions)

GMAT CAT - Graduate Management Admission Test

LSAT - Law School Admission Test

MAT - Miller Analogies Test

MCAT - Medical College Admission Test

MTEL - Massachusetts Tests for Educator Licensure

NJ HSPA - New Jersey High School Proficiency Assessment

NYSTCE: LAST & ATS-W - New York State Teacher Certification

PLT - Principles of Learning & Teaching Tests

PPST - Pre-Professional Skills Tests

PSAT - Preliminary Scholastic Assessment Test

SAT

TExES - Texas Examinations of Educator Standards

THEA - Texas Higher Education Assessment

TOEFL - Test of English as a Foreign Language

TOEIC - Test of English for International Communication

USMLE Steps 1,2,3 - U.S. Medical Licensing Exams

U.S. Postal Exams 460 & 470

RESEARCH & EDUCATION ASSOCIATION
61 Ethel Road W. • Piscataway, New Jersey 08854
Phone: (732) 819-8880   **website: www.rea.com**

Please send me more information about your Test Prep books

Name _____

Address _____

City _____ State _____ Zip _____